100
DISHES FOR SLIMMERS

100 DISHES FOR SLIMMERS

Edited by
Diane Leah

OCTOPUS BOOKS

CONTENTS

NOTES

Standard spoon measurements are used in all recipes
1 tablespoon = one 15 ml spoon
1 teaspoon = one 5 ml spoon
All spoon measures are level
Where amounts of salt and pepper are not specified,
the cook should use her own discretion.
Canned foods should not be drained, unless so stated
in the recipe.
For all recipes, quantities are given in metric, imperial
and American measures. Follow one set of measures only,
because they are not interchangeable.
Ovens should be preheated to the specified temperature.

First published 1985 by
Octopus Books Limited
59 Grosvenor St, London W1

© 1985 Octopus Books Limited

ISBN 0 7064 2316 X

Produced by Mandarin Publishers Ltd
22a Westlands Rd
Quarry Bay, Hong Kong

Printed in Hong Kong

Frontispiece
Minted Grapefruit (page 12)
Cucumber and Fennel Salad (page 40)
Scampi Provençale (page 16)

INTRODUCTION

Successful slimming and the maintenance of a suitable target weight need not be a penance. Often a diet is seen merely as a short period of deprivation that results in the loss of a few kilos/pounds. These crash or cranky diets may be successful in the short term but they will always fail in the long run because they don't have a lasting effect on your eating habits. Without a change in your eating habits it is only a matter of time before all the weight you lose creeps back on again. Dieting should, in fact, be a gradual process and the weight lost should be as a result of a permanent change in your eating habits.

One way that eating habits can be improved is by cutting down on the amount of fat in your diet. Quite apart from reducing the risk of all the health problems that are linked with a high-fat diet, a low-fat diet will automatically reduce the number of calories consumed. Substitute skimmed milk for whole-fat milk and experiment with the low-fat spreads which are now on the market.

Avoid baked goods, such as cakes, biscuits and pastries which are usually high in both hidden fat and sugar and choose cooking methods like steaming, poaching or grilling (broiling) rather than frying. A boiled or poached egg has only 80 calories, but if that same egg is fried its calorie count shoots up to 135. If you really do have a yearning for chips (French fries), try the 'cheat' chips on page 40. They have a similar flavour but less than half the calories.

Reduce the amount of sugar in your diet. Refined sugar has no nutritive value other than extra energy provided by its high calorie content. Stop taking sugar in tea or coffee, use a sugar substitute if necessary, and beware of soft drinks which are often little more than sugar, water and colouring. Drink pure fruit juices mixed with mineral water instead.

Fresh fruit and vegetables are an invaluable part of any healthy eating plan. Their nutritive value is high and their calorie content low, so eat plenty of them. Remember, however, that the way you prepare them will affect their calorie content. Resist the temptation to add that knob of butter to vegetables before serving.

Foods which are high in fibre are also a good choice for slimmers. Although they in themselves may not be particularly 'low-calorie' foods, they are usually very filling, so you don't need to eat a lot of them. High-fibre foods include wholegrain cereals, pulses and wholewheat bread. Although traditionally considered 'fattening' foods, it is a mistake to cut out bread and potatoes as they are both filling and satisfying. It is more often what is put on them, or how they are cooked, that has led to them being thought of as 'high-calorie' foods. Jacket potatoes, for example, are cheap and filling and can be filled with a variety of low-calorie foods to make them more exciting (see page 43).

When eating out, avoid dishes which are cooked in or served with rich sauces. Choose simply cooked dishes, like grilled (broiled) fish or chicken served with vegetables or a crisp undressed salad.

A sweet tooth is many a dieter's downfall. If you really can't deny your craving for sweet things, experiment with artificial sweeteners. There are several on the market now which do not have that bitter after-taste associated with saccharin. If you are using an artificial sweetener in a dish which requires cooking, check that the sweetener is suitable, some break down and lose their sweetness when heated. Alternatively, use foods that provide natural sweetness, such as dates or other dried fruits, which also supply valuable dietary fibre, but remember their calorie value can be very high.

Try to involve the whole family with your better way of eating. They will all benefit from a high-fibre, low-fat and low-sugar diet. Offer your children low-calorie snacks like fresh fruit and fruit drinks rather than their sticky alternatives. Give schoolchildren well-balanced packed lunches, rather than money which will invariably be spent at the local chip shop or tuck shop giving rise to bad eating habits. Never force children to eat fruit and vegetables – when they see how much you are enjoying them, they will wonder what they are missing and want to try them for themselves. Don't reward young children by giving them sweets – give them a hug instead!

Once you have lost a little weight, you will feel more attractive, your clothes will fit again and you will generally be fitter and more energetic.

Start by counting the calories in everything you eat; the recipes in this book will help you to produce interesting meals which are already calorie counted for you. After a while you will automatically know which foods to choose and which to avoid and your new eating plan will become a way of life.

SOUPS AND STARTERS

Tomato Soup with Basil

METRIC/IMPERIAL	AMERICAN
50 g/2 oz low-fat spread	¼ cup low-fat spread
1 large mild onion, chopped	1 large mild onion, chopped
675 g/1½ lb tomatoes	1½ lb tomatoes
600 ml/1 pint hot chicken stock	2½ cups hot chicken stock
salt	salt
freshly ground black pepper	freshly ground black pepper
pinch of sugar	pinch of sugar
3 tablespoons chopped fresh basil	3 tablespoons chopped fresh basil

Melt the spread in a saucepan and cook the onion gently until soft but not coloured. Skin the tomatoes, chop them and add to the onion. Stir for a few minutes in the spread, then pour on the heated stock. Bring to the boil, then lower the heat and simmer for 20 minutes, adding salt, pepper and a pinch of sugar.

Purée briefly in a blender, or pass through a sieve. Adjust the seasoning, cool, and chill well. Ten minutes before serving, stir in the chopped basil.
Serves 4
Total Calories 395
98 Calories per portion

Jellied Cucumber and Mint Soup

METRIC/IMPERIAL	AMERICAN
1 shallot, peeled	1 shallot, peeled
1 cucumber	1 cucumber
900 ml/1½ pints chicken stock	3¾ cups chicken stock
salt	salt
freshly ground black pepper	freshly ground black pepper
2 tablespoons lemon juice	2 tablespoons lemon juice
1 tablespoon gelatine	1 envelope gelatin
3 tablespoons chopped mint	3 tablespoons chopped mint
lemon quarters to serve	lemon quarters to serve

Chop the peeled shallot finely. Remove about half the skin of the cucumber and discard. Grate the remaining cucumber coarsely, squeezing out the juice. Heat the stock and cook the chopped shallot for 4 minutes. Add the grated cucumber and salt and pepper to taste. Stir in the lemon juice.

Dissolve the gelatine in a little of the stock; when dissolved, strain and return to the rest of the soup. Leave to cool. When half-set, stir in the finely chopped mint. Chill again.

To serve, spoon into cups – it is not meant to be a firm jelly – and serve with lemon quarters.
Serves 4
Total Calories 160
40 Calories per portion

Tomato Soup with Basil
Jellied Cucumber and Mint Soup

Curried Mushroom Salad

METRIC/IMPERIAL	AMERICAN
225 g/8 oz button mushrooms, sliced	2 cups sliced button mushrooms
100 g/4 oz cooked ham, chopped	½ cup chopped cooked ham
100 g/4 oz cucumber, diced	1 cup diced cucumber
150 ml/¼ pint plain yogurt	⅔ cup plain yogurt
1 tablespoon concentrated curry sauce or 1 teaspoon curry powder	1 tablespoon concentrated curry sauce or 1 teaspoon curry powder
2 teaspoons lemon juice	2 teaspoons lemon juice
salt	salt
freshly ground black pepper	freshly ground black pepper
2 tablespoons mango chutney	2 tablespoons mango chutney
shredded lettuce to garnish	shredded lettuce to garnish

Mix the mushrooms, ham and cucumber together in a bowl. Combine the yogurt, curry, lemon juice and salt and pepper in a separate bowl. Chop any large pieces of mango in the chutney and add to the yogurt mixture. Pour over the the mushrooms and stir until well coated. Chill for 1 to 2 hours in the refrigerator. Serve garnished with shredded lettuce.
Serves 4
Total Calories 410
102 Calories per portion

Spiced Grapefruit Cups

METRIC/IMPERIAL	AMERICAN
1 grapefruit	1 grapefruit
25 g/1 oz Sultana Bran cereal	¾ cup Golden Raisin Bran cereal
½ teaspoon mixed spice	½ teaspoon ground allspice

Cut the grapefruit in half and scoop out the flesh over a bowl to catch any juice. Roughly chop the flesh in the bowl and add all but 2 teaspoons of the Sultana (Golden Raisin) Bran, and the mixed spice (ground allspice). Spoon the mixture into the grapefruit halves and sprinkle with the remaining cereal. Bake in a preheated moderately hot oven (200°C/400°F, Gas Mark 6) for 15 minutes. Serve hot.
Serves 2
Total Calories 120
60 Calories per portion

Artichoke Cocktail

METRIC/IMPERIAL	AMERICAN
2 cooked globe artichokes	2 cooked globe artichokes
150 ml/¼ pint plain yogurt	⅔ cup plain yogurt
1 tablespoon chopped fresh chives	1 tablespoon chopped fresh chives
1 tablespoon chopped fresh parsley	1 tablespoon chopped fresh parsley
1 teaspoon chopped capers	1 teaspoon chopped capers
pinch of cayenne pepper	pinch of cayenne pepper
pinch of garlic salt	pinch of garlic salt
½ teaspoon dried tarragon	½ teaspoon dried tarragon
25 g/1 oz peeled prawns	2 tablespoons shelled shrimp
salt	salt
fresh ground black pepper	freshly ground black pepper
To garnish:	**To garnish:**
few whole prawns	few whole shrimp
lemon slices	lemon slices

Cool the artichokes and remove the chokes. Mix the yogurt with the remaining ingredients and divide the sauce between the two artichokes. Chill in the refrigerator for at least 1 hour before serving. Garnish with whole prawns (shrimp) and lemon slices.
Serves 2
Total Calories 140
70 Calories per portion

Prawn and Pineapple Cocktail

METRIC/IMPERIAL	AMERICAN
1 small fresh pineapple, peeled and diced	1 small fresh pineapple, peeled and diced
225 g/8 oz black grapes	½ lb purple grapes
450 g/1 lb peeled prawns	1 lb shelled shrimp
4 tablespoons low-calorie mayonnaise	4 tablespoons low-calorie mayonnaise
2 tablespoons plain yogurt	2 tablespoons plain yogurt
salt	salt
freshly ground black pepper	freshly ground black pepper
lettuce to serve	lettuce to serve

Mix the pineapple, grapes, prawns (shrimp) and mayonnaise with the yogurt and salt and pepper to taste. Serve on a bed of lettuce.
Serves 4 to 6
Total Calories 895
224 to 149 Calories per portion

Pilchard and Dill Pâté

METRIC/IMPERIAL	AMERICAN
1 × 425 g/15 oz can pilchards in brine	1 × 15 oz can pilchards in brine
50 g/2 oz low-fat spread	¼ cup low-fat spread
50 g/2 oz low-fat curd cheese	¼ cup low-fat small curd cottage cheese
25 g/1 oz fresh white breadcrumbs	½ cup soft white bread crumbs
1 teaspoon chopped fresh dill	1 teaspoon chopped fresh dill
½ teaspoon Tabasco sauce or pinch of cayenne pepper	½ teaspoon hot pepper sauce or pinch of cayenne pepper
salt	salt
freshly ground black pepper	freshly ground black pepper
1 tablespoon lemon juice	1 tablespoon lemon juice

Drain the pilchards and place in a blender or food processor with the remaining ingredients. Process until smooth. Taste and adjust the seasoning, as necessary. Place in six individual ramekin dishes and chill before serving.
Serves 6
Total Calories 975
163 Calories per portion

Mushroom Hors d'oeuvre

METRIC/IMPERIAL	AMERICAN
150 ml/¼ pint plain yogurt	⅔ cup plain yogurt
1 tablespoon tomato purée	1 tablespoon tomato paste
1 tablespoon finely chopped chives or spring onions	1 tablespoon finely chopped chives or scallions
salt	salt
freshly ground black pepper	freshly ground black pepper
225 g/8 oz button mushrooms	2 cups button mushrooms
To serve:	**To serve:**
chicory or lettuce leaves	endive or lettuce leaves
crispbreads	crispbreads

Mix together the yogurt, tomato purée (paste), chives or onions (scallions) and salt and pepper to taste. Stir in the mushrooms and serve on a bed of chicory (endive) or lettuce leaves, with a selection of crispbreads.
Serves 2
Total Calories 120
60 Calories per portion

Chicken Liver Pâté

METRIC/IMPERIAL	AMERICAN
15 g/½ oz butter	1 tablespoon butter
1 onion, chopped	1 onion, chopped
225 g/8 oz chicken livers	½ lb chicken livers
½ teaspoon dried mixed herbs	½ teaspoon dried mixed herbs
½ teaspoon French mustard	½ teaspoon Dijon-style mustard
2 tablespoons red wine or sherry	2 tablespoons red wine or sherry
225 g/8 oz cottage cheese	1 cup cottage cheese
melba toast or wholewheat bread to serve	melba toast or wholewheat bread to serve

Melt the butter in a saucepan and sauté the onion and chicken livers until the livers change colour. Add the mixed herbs, mustard and wine and cook for a further 5 minutes. Remove from the heat and leave to cool.

Place the liver mixture in a blender or food processor with the cottage cheese and process until smooth. Spoon into a small pot, cover and refrigerate until required. Serve with melba toast or wholewheat bread, but no butter.
Serves 4
Total Calories 675 (without toast or bread)
169 Calories per portion (without toast or bread)

Tomato, Orange and Celery Soup

METRIC/IMPERIAL	AMERICAN
600 ml/1 pint chicken stock	2½ cups chicken stock
3 celery sticks, finely chopped	3 stalks celery, finely chopped
400 ml/14 fl oz tomato juice	1¾ cups tomato juice
2 tomatoes, peeled, seeded and chopped	2 tomatoes, peeled, seeded and chopped
1 tablespoon Worcestershire sauce	1 tablespoon Worcestershire sauce
grated rind and juice of 1 orange	grated rind and juice of 1 orange
1 teaspoon dried sweet basil	1 teaspoon dried sweet basil

Place the chicken stock and celery in a large saucepan. Bring to the boil, cover and simmer for 10 minutes. Add the remaining ingredients and simmer for a further 5 minutes, until the celery and tomato are soft. Serve hot.
Serves 4
Total Calories 190
47 Calories per portion

Melon and Mint Sorbet

METRIC/IMPERIAL	AMERICAN
600 ml/1 pint water	2½ cups water
100 g/4 oz caster sugar	½ cup superfine sugar
1 tablespoon lemon juice	1 tablespoon lemon juice
2 sprigs fresh mint, chopped	2 sprigs fresh mint, chopped
1 honeydew melon	1 honeydew melon
1 teaspoon peppermint essence	1 teaspoon peppermint extract
2 egg whites	2 egg whites

Put the water, sugar and lemon juice in a heavy-based pan. Heat gently until the sugar has dissolved. Increase the heat and cook rapidly until thread stage is reached. Dip thumb and finger in cold water, then very quickly in the syrup. Press thumb and finger together, pull apart and a fine thread should be formed. Remove from the heat and stir in the chopped mint. Cool.

Scoop the flesh from the melon, remove the pips and liquidize to a purée. Alternatively, rub through a sieve. Stir into the sugar syrup with the peppermint essence (extract). Pour the mixture into a freezer container and freeze for about 1½ hours until mushy, stirring occasionally.

Beat the egg whites until they form soft peaks. Fold into the mixture and freeze. Beat the mixture twice, at hourly intervals. Cover, seal and freeze.
Serves 4 to 6
Total Calories 565
141 to 94 Calories per portion

Tomato Sorbet

METRIC/IMPERIAL	AMERICAN
100 g/4 oz caster sugar	½ cup superfine sugar
300 ml/½ pint water	1¼ cups water
300 ml/½ pint tomato juice	1¼ cups tomato juice
juice of ½ lemon	juice of ½ lemon
1 teaspoon Worcestershire sauce	1 teaspoon Worcestershire sauce
6 drops Tabasco sauce	6 drops hot pepper sauce
1 teaspoon soy sauce	1 teaspoon soy sauce
salt	salt
freshly ground black pepper	freshly ground black pepper
2 egg whites	2 egg whites
To serve:	**To serve:**
6 large ripe tomatoes	6 large ripe tomatoes
fresh coriander leaves	fresh coriander leaves

Put the sugar and water in a heavy-based pan and heat gently until the sugar has dissolved. Increase the heat and cook rapidly until thread stage is reached. Dip thumb and finger in cold water, then very quickly in the syrup. Press thumb and finger together, pull apart and a thread should be formed. Leave to cool.

Stir in the tomato juice, lemon juice, Worcestershire, Tabasco (hot pepper) and soy sauces. Add salt and pepper to taste. Pour into a freezer container and freeze for about 1½ hours until mushy, stirring occasionally.

Beat the egg whites until they form soft peaks and fold into the tomato mixture. Cover, seal and freeze. To serve, allow the sorbet to defrost for about 45 minutes at room temperature. Halve the tomatoes with zigzag cuts, and scoop out the flesh and pips. Fill with scoops of the sorbet and garnish with sprigs of coriander.
Makes 12
Total Calories 595
50 Calories per portion

Cucumber Sorbet

METRIC/IMPERIAL	AMERICAN
1 teaspoon gelatine	½ envelope gelatin
300 ml/½ pint water	1¼ cups water
50 g/2 oz sugar	¼ cup sugar
juice of ½ lemon	juice of ½ lemon
2 firm eating apples	2 firm dessert apples
1 large cucumber, peeled and cut into chunks	1 large cucumber, peeled and cut into chunks
½ teaspoon dried dill	½ teaspoon dried dill
salt	salt
freshly ground black pepper	freshly ground black pepper
2 egg whites	2 egg whites
To serve:	**To serve:**
6 prawns in their shell	6 shrimp in their shell
fresh dill sprigs	fresh dill sprigs

Put the gelatine and 2 tablespoons of the water in a small bowl and leave to soak.

Put the sugar and the remaining water in a heavy-based pan. Heat gently until the sugar has dissolved. Increase the heat and cook rapidly for 3 minutes. Allow to cool slightly then pour the syrup over the gelatine and stir gently until the gelatine has completely dissolved. Stir in the lemon juice and cool.

Peel and core the apples. Cut into chunks and liquidize with the cucumber and the sugar syrup. Add the dill, and salt and pepper to taste. Pour the mixture into a freezer container and freeze for about 1½ hours until mushy, stirring occasionally.

Beat the egg whites until they form soft peaks and fold into the mixture. Cover, seal and freeze.

Serve garnished with prawns (shrimp) and dill.
Serves 6
Total Calories 440
73 Calories per portion

Cucumber Sorbet
Melon and Mint Sorbet
Tomato Sorbet

Minted Grapefruit

METRIC/IMPERIAL	AMERICAN
2 large grapefruit	2 large grapefruit
2 oranges	2 oranges
1 tablespoon lemon juice	1 tablespoon lemon juice
1 × 240 ml/8½ fl oz bottle low-calorie lemonade	1 cup low-calorie lemonade
2 tablespoons finely chopped fresh mint	2 tablespoons finely chopped fresh mint
4 mint sprigs to finish	4 mint sprigs to finish

Halve the grapefruit, using a zig-zag cut to give a decorative edge. Remove the flesh from the halves. Peel and segment the oranges, remove the membranes and cut the segments into pieces. Mix with the grapefruit and return to the grapefruit shells.

Mix together the lemon juice, lemonade and chopped mint. Pour into an ice tray and freeze until mushy. Pile on top of the grapefruit and decorate with a sprig of mint. Serve immediately.

Serves 4
Total Calories 220
55 Calories per portion

Courgettes (Zucchini) with Mushrooms and Smoked Salmon

METRIC/IMPERIAL	AMERICAN
225 g/8 oz courgettes, thinly sliced	½ lb zucchini, thinly sliced
100 g/4 oz mushrooms, sliced	1 cup sliced mushrooms
100 g/4 oz smoked salmon, cut into thin strips	½ cup smoked salmon, cut into thin strips
2 tablespoons lemon juice	2 tablespoons lemon juice
1 clove garlic, crushed (optional)	1 clove garlic, crushed (optional)
celery salt	celery salt
freshly ground black pepper	freshly ground black pepper
lemon wedges to garnish	lemon wedges to garnish

Mix together the courgettes (zucchini), mushrooms and salmon. Mix the remaining ingredients, except the lemon wedges. Just before serving, pour over the salmon mixture and toss well. Garnish with lemon wedges.

Serves 2
Total Calories 210
105 Calories per portion

Scandinavian Sardine Snack

METRIC/IMPERIAL	AMERICAN
50 g/2 oz cucumber, finely chopped	½ cup finely chopped cucumber
½ teaspoon salt	½ teaspoon salt
2 slices pumpernickel bread	2 slices pumpernickel bread
low-fat spread	low-fat spread
lettuce leaves	lettuce leaves
1 × 120 g/4 oz can sardines in oil	1 × 4 oz can sardines in oil
1 tablespoon finely chopped onion	1 tablespoon finely chopped onion
2 tablespoons plain yogurt	2 tablespoons plain yogurt
Worcestershire sauce	Worcestershire sauce
To garnish:	**To garnish:**
twist of lemon	twist of lemon
paprika	paprika

Place the cucumber in a sieve and sprinkle with the salt. Leave to drain for about 30 minutes. Spread the pumpernickel slices with low-fat spread and arrange the lettuce leaves on top. Drain the oil from the sardines then remove further oil by putting the sardines on kitchen paper towels. Arrange the fish on the lettuce. Squeeze excess moisture from the cucumber and mix with the onion, yogurt and Worcestershire sauce. Spoon on top of the sardines and garnish with a twist of lemon and paprika.

Serves 2
Total Calories 435
217 Calories per portion

Chilled Carrot Soup

METRIC/IMPERIAL	AMERICAN
2 tablespoons vegetable oil	2 tablespoons vegetable oil
1 large onion, chopped	1 large onion, chopped
1½ teaspoons curry powder	1½ teaspoons curry powder
900 ml/1½ pints chicken stock	3¾ cups chicken stock
450 g/1 lb carrots, sliced	1 lb carrots, sliced
2 sticks celery, sliced	2 stalks celery, sliced
1 bay leaf	1 bay leaf
½ teaspoon ground cumin	½ teaspoon ground cumin
½ teaspoon Tabasco sauce	½ teaspoon hot pepper sauce
250 ml/8 fl oz skimmed milk	1 cup skim milk
225 g/8 oz cottage cheese	1 cup cottage cheese

Heat the oil in a large saucepan. Sauté the onion and curry powder over a medium heat for 3 to 5 minutes. Add the stock, carrots, celery, bay leaf, cumin and Tabasco (hot pepper) sauce. Bring to the boil, reduce the heat and simmer until all the vegetables are tender. Remove the bay leaf, leave the soup to cool slightly, then transfer to a blender or food processor. Process for about 1 minute until smooth. Pour into a bowl and leave to cool.

Place the milk and cottage cheese in the blender or food processor and process briefly until smooth. Stir into the soup and chill in the refrigerator before serving.
Serves 6
Total Calories 720
120 Calories per portion

Quick Kipper Mousse

METRIC/IMPERIAL	AMERICAN
15 g/½ oz low-fat spread	1 tablespoon low-fat spread
1 small onion, chopped	1 small onion, chopped
1 × 175 g/6 oz packet frozen kipper fillets, cooked, skinned and flaked	1 × 6 oz packet frozen kipper fillets, cooked, skinned and flaked
225 g/8 oz cottage cheese, sieved	1 cup cottage cheese, sieved
150 ml/¼ pint water	⅔ cup water
15 g/½ oz powdered gelatine	2 envelopes unflavored gelatin
salt	salt
freshly ground black pepper	freshly ground black pepper
To garnish:	**To garnish:**
cucumber slices	cucumber slices
watercress	watercress

Melt the low-fat spread in a saucepan and sauté the onion until soft. Stir together the onion, kippers and cottage cheese. Put the water in a heatproof bowl and sprinkle over the gelatine. Stir briskly and stand the bowl over hot water until the gelatine has dissolved. Beat well into the fish mixture, or place the fish mixture and gelatine in a blender or food processor and process briefly. Add salt and pepper to taste. Pour into a greased 500 g/1 lb loaf tin (7 × 3 inch loaf pan), and leave to set. Turn out and garnish with cucumber slices and watercress.
Serves 4
Total Calories 685
171 Calories per portion

FISH DISHES

Smoked Mackerel Salad

METRIC/IMPERIAL	AMERICAN
½ cucumber	½ cucumber
salt	salt
4 to 6 tablespoons beansprouts	4 to 6 tablespoons bean sprouts
5 tablespoons low calorie dressing	5 tablespoons low calorie dressing
4 firm tomatoes, peeled, seeded and diced	4 firm tomatoes, peeled, seeded and diced
4 small smoked mackerel fillets	4 small smoked mackerel fillets

Cut the cucumber into 5 mm/¼ inch dice, mix with 1 teaspoon salt and leave in a colander to drain for 30 minutes.

Rinse the beansprouts in cold water, drain thoroughly and chill in the refrigerator until ready to serve.

Rinse the cucumber under cold water and pat dry, then add to the dressing with the tomato and beansprouts and toss lightly together.

Arrange the fillets of fish on individual serving dishes and serve with the salad.
Serves 4
Total Calories 640
160 Calories per portion

Fish and Pasta Creole

METRIC/IMPERIAL	AMERICAN
25 g/1 oz butter	2 tablespoons butter
1 clove garlic, crushed (optional)	1 clove garlic, crushed (optional)
2-3 celery sticks, chopped	2-3 stalks celery, chopped
1 × 400 g/14 oz can tomatoes	1 × 14 oz can tomatoes
300 ml/½ pint fish or chicken stock	1¼ cups fish or chicken stock
100 g/4 oz short-cut macaroni	1 cup elbow macaroni
1 bay leaf	1 bay leaf
175 g/6 oz sweetcorn	1 cup whole kernel corn
750 g/1½ lb coley or monkfish, skinned and cubed	1½ lb coley or other white fish, skinned and cubed
salt	salt
freshly ground black pepper	freshly ground black pepper
1 tablespoon chopped fresh parsley to garnish	1 tablespoon chopped fresh parsley to garnish

Melt the butter in a large saucepan and lightly sauté the garlic (if using) and celery. Add the tomatoes, stock, pasta and bay leaf. Cover and simmer for 5 to 6 minutes. Add the sweetcorn (whole kernel corn) and fish. Season to taste and simmer gently for another 5 to 6 minutes, until the fish and pasta are tender. Remove the bay leaf and serve hot, garnished with chopped parsley.
Serves 4
Total Calories 1360
340 Calories per portion

Smoked Mackerel Salad

Slimmers' Haddock and Cider Casserole

METRIC/IMPERIAL	AMERICAN
1 small onion, finely chopped	1 small onion, finely chopped
100 g/4 oz button mushrooms, sliced	1 cup button mushrooms, sliced
1 × 425 g/15 oz can tomatoes, drained	1 × 15 oz can tomatoes, drained
1 tablespoon chopped fresh parsley	1 tablespoon chopped fresh parsley
1 teaspoon dried sweet basil	1 teaspoon dried sweet basil
15 g/½ oz flour	2 tablespoons flour
750 g/1½ lb haddock fillets, skinned	1½ lb haddock fillets, skinned
salt	salt
freshly ground black pepper	freshly ground black pepper
120 ml/4 fl oz dry cider	½ cup hard cider
Topping:	**Topping:**
75 g/3 oz fresh wholewheat breadcrumbs	1½ cups soft wholewheat bread crumbs
100 g/4 oz Edam cheese, grated	1 cup grated Edam cheese

Place the onion, mushrooms and tomatoes in a large ovenproof dish and sprinkle over the herbs and flour. Divide the fish into four portions, season with salt and pepper and roll up. Put on top of the vegetable mixture and pour over the cider. Mix together the topping ingredients and spoon over the fish. Bake in a preheated moderate oven (180°C/350°F, Gas Mark 4) for 35 minutes.
Serves 4
Total Calories 1210
302 Calories per portion

Harvest Pilchards

METRIC/IMPERIAL	AMERICAN
175 g/6 oz potatoes, peeled and thinly sliced	1 cup peeled and thinly sliced potatoes
225 g/8 oz apples, cored and thinly sliced	½ lb apples, cored and thinly sliced
1 × 425 g/15 oz can pilchards in brine	1 × 15 oz can pilchards in brine
2 teaspoons grated lemon rind	2 teaspoons grated lemon rind
300 ml/½ pint cider	1¼ cups cider
4 tomatoes, sliced	4 tomatoes, sliced

Cook the potatoes in boiling salted water for 2 to 3 minutes only, making sure they are still firm, then drain. Place the apples and the pilchards with brine in a saucepan and cook gently for 10 minutes. Transfer to a casserole, add the lemon rind and top with the slices of potato. Pour over the cider and arrange the tomato slices on top. Cover and bake in a preheated moderate oven (180°C/350°F, Gas Mark 4) for 45 minutes.
Serves 4
Total Calories 740
185 Calories per portion

Scampi Provençale

METRIC/IMPERIAL	AMERICAN
1 tablespoon oil	1 tablespoon oil
1 small onion, peeled and finely chopped	1 small onion, peeled and finely chopped
1 clove garlic, finely chopped	1 clove garlic, finely chopped
3 tomatoes, peeled and finely chopped	3 tomatoes, peeled and finely chopped
450 g/1 lb scampi	1 lb scampi
chopped parsley	chopped parsley
little white wine	little white wine
salt	salt
freshly ground black pepper	freshly ground black pepper
lemon slices (optional)	lemon slices (optional)
parsley sprigs (optional)	parsley sprigs (optional)

Heat the oil and sauté the onion and garlic in it. Add the tomatoes, scampi, parsley and white wine to moisten. Cook steadily for 5 to 6 minutes. Season to taste and serve hot, garnished with lemon slices and parsley sprigs if liked.
Serves 4
Total Calories 680
170 Calories per portion

Barbecued Fish Kebabs (Kabobs)

METRIC/IMPERIAL	AMERICAN
4 mackerel or herring, cleaned and boned	4 mackerel or herring, cleaned and boned
3 small onions, quartered	3 small onions, quartered
4 tomatoes, halved	4 tomatoes, halved
300 g/11 oz boiled rice to serve	2 cups boiled rice to serve
Sauce:	**Sauce:**
300 ml/½ pint fish or chicken stock	1¼ cups fish or chicken stock
150 ml/¼ pint tomato ketchup	⅔ cup ketchup
2 tablespoons Worcestershire sauce	2 tablespoons Worcestershire sauce
2 tablespoons wine vinegar	2 tablespoons wine vinegar
1 tablespoon brown sugar or few drops liquid sweetener	1 tablespoon brown sugar or few drops liquid sweetener
2 drops Tabasco sauce (optional)	2 drops hot pepper sauce (optional)
2 tablespoons tomato purée	2 tablespoons tomato paste
salt	salt
freshly ground black pepper	freshly ground black pepper
1 tablespoon cornflour	1 tablespoon cornstarch

Cut each fish crosswise into four. To make the sauce, mix together all the ingredients, except the cornflour (cornstarch), in a large bowl. Add the fish and leave to marinate for about 1 hour.

Drain the fish, reserving the marinade, and thread the fish on to skewers, alternating with the onions and tomatoes. Grill (broil) for 10 minutes, basting with the sauce and turning the skewers frequently. Meanwhile, blend the cornflour (cornstarch) with a little water to make a smooth paste. Add to the remaining sauce, together with any juices from the grill (broiler) pan, and bring to the boil in a saucepan, stirring well. Serve the kebabs (kabobs) on a bed of rice accompanied by the sauce.

Serves 2 to 4
Total Calories 1715
857 to 429 Calories per portion

Tuna and Broccoli Golden Bake

METRIC/IMPERIAL	AMERICAN
1 × 250 g/8 oz packet frozen broccoli, cooked	1 × 8 oz packet frozen broccoli, cooked
25 g/1 oz low-fat spread	2 tablespoons low-fat spread
1 × 200 g/7 oz can tuna in brine, drained and flaked	1 × 7 oz can tuna in brine, drained and flaked
2 tomatoes, quartered	2 tomatoes, quartered
salt	salt
freshly ground black pepper	freshly ground black pepper
Cheese sauce:	**Cheese sauce:**
25 g/1 oz low-fat spread	2 tablespoons low-fat spread
25 g/1 oz flour	¼ cup flour
250 ml/8 fl oz skimmed milk	1 cup skim milk
salt	salt
freshly ground black pepper	freshly ground black pepper
pinch of dry mustard	pinch of dry mustard
100 g/4 oz Edam cheese, grated	1 cup grated Edam cheese

Arrange the cooked broccoli in the bottom of an ovenproof dish and dot with low-fat spread. Place the tuna and the tomatoes on top and add salt and pepper to taste.

To make the sauce, place all the ingredients, except the cheese, in a saucepan. Bring to the boil, whisking all the time, and simmer until the sauce thickens. Add three-quarters of the cheese and pour over the tuna and tomato, leaving a border of broccoli showing around the edge. Sprinkle with the remaining cheese and bake in a preheated moderately hot oven (200°C/400°F, Gas Mark 6) until golden brown. Serve hot.

Serves 2
Total Calories 1185
592 Calories per portion

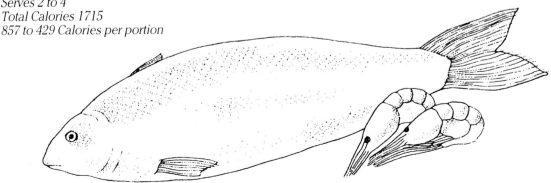

Crab Stuffed Cucumbers

METRIC/IMPERIAL	AMERICAN
2 large cucumbers, halved lengthwise and seeded	2 large cucumbers, halved lengthwise and seeded
2 × 185 g/6½ oz cans crabmeat, drained	2 × 6½ oz cans crab meat, drained
2 tablespoons finely chopped onion	2 tablespoons finely chopped onion
2 small carrots, cut into thin strips	2 small carrots, cut into thin strips
2 tablespoons tarragon vinegar	2 tablespoons tarragon vinegar
½ teaspoon dried tarragon	½ teaspoon dried tarragon
120 ml/4 fl oz low-fat yogurt	½ cup low-fat yogurt
cayenne pepper	cayenne
salt	salt
To garnish:	**To garnish:**
tomato wedges	tomato wedges
parsley sprigs	parsley sprigs

Scoop the flesh out of the cucumber halves, leaving a shell about 3 mm/⅛ inch thick. Set aside. Chop the flesh and place in a mixing bowl with the crabmeat, onion, carrots, vinegar, tarragon and yogurt and season with cayenne and salt. Mix together well.

Spoon the mixture into the reserved cucumber shells. Cover loosely and chill in the refrigerator for 1 to 2 hours. Serve garnished with tomato and parsley.
Serves 4
Total Calories 516
129 Calories per portion

Herring and Yogurt Salad

METRIC/IMPERIAL	AMERICAN
4 herring, cleaned and boned	4 herring, cleaned and boned
1 onion, thinly sliced	1 onion, thinly sliced
1 teaspoon dried tarragon	1 teaspoon dried tarragon
6 peppercorns	6 peppercorns
salt	salt
150 ml/¼ pint fish or chicken stock	⅔ cup fish or chicken stock
150 ml/¼ pint wine vinegar	⅔ cup wine vinegar
150 ml/¼ pint plain yogurt	⅔ cup plain yogurt
To garnish:	**To garnish:**
1 dessert apple	1 dessert apple
1 tablespoon lemon juice	1 tablespoon lemon juice

Roll up the herring from head to tail and secure each with a wooden cocktail stick (toothpick). Place the fish

in a shallow ovenproof dish and cover with the onion slices, tarragon, peppercorns, salt, stock and vinegar. Cover and bake in a preheated moderate oven (160°C/325°F, Gas Mark 3) for 30 minutes. Remove from the oven, leave to cool, then chill in the refrigerator.

Just before serving, drain the fish, reserving the liquid, and arrange on a serving dish. Strain the liquid and blend 2 tablespoons with the yogurt. Pour the yogurt mixture over the fish. Core and slice the apple, dip in lemon juice and use to garnish the fish.
Serves 2 to 4
Total Calories 1085
542 to 271 Calories per portion

Prawn (Shrimp) and Pineapple Kebabs (Kabobs)

METRIC/IMPERIAL	AMERICAN
120 ml/4 fl oz soy sauce	½ cup soy sauce
120 ml/4 fl oz sherry	½ cup sherry
2 teaspoons sesame oil	2 teaspoons sesame oil
1 tablespoon minced fresh root ginger	1 tablespoons minced fresh ginger root
1 clove garlic, crushed	1 clove garlic, crushed
450 g/1 lb large prawns, peeled (about 24)	1 lb raw shrimp (about 24), shelled and deveined
½ fresh pineapple, peeled, cored and cut into wedges	½ fresh pineapple, peeled, cored and cut into wedges
450 g/1 lb Brussels sprouts	1 lb Brussels sprouts
salt	salt
2 red peppers, cored, seeded and cut into 2.5 cm/1 inch squares	2 red peppers, cored, seeded and cut into 1 inch squares

Combine the soy sauce, sherry, sesame oil, root ginger and garlic in a shallow bowl. Place the prawns (shrimp) and pineapple chunks in the mixture and leave to marinate for 3 to 4 hours, turning occasionally.

Blanch the Brussels sprouts in boiling salted water for 1 to 2 minutes; drain.

Drain the prawns (shrimp) and pineapple, reserving the marinade. Thread the prawns (shrimp), pineapple, Brussels sprouts and peppers onto four metal skewers, alternating ingredients, ending with a sprout.

Brush with the reserved marinade and grill (broil) under a preheated grill (broiler) for 3 to 4 minutes, turning once and brushing with the marinade. Grill (broil) until the fish is just cooked through.
Serves 4
Total Calories 864
216 Calories per portion

Prawn (Shrimp) and Pineapple Kebabs (Kabobs)
Crab Stuffed Cucumber

Plaice (Flounder) with Peaches

METRIC/IMPERIAL	AMERICAN
4 × 175 g/6 oz plaice fillets, skinned	4 × 6 oz flounder fillets, skinned
grated rind and juice of 1 lemon	grated rind and juice of 1 lemon
1 × 300 g/10 oz can peach slices in natural juice	1 × 10 oz can peach slices in natural juice
8 button mushrooms, sliced	8 button mushrooms, sliced
salt	salt
freshly ground black pepper	freshly ground black pepper

Place the fish in an ovenproof dish and add the lemon rind and juice, peach juice, mushrooms and salt and pepper to taste.
Cover and bake in a preheated moderate oven (180°C/350°F, Gas Mark 4) for 30 minutes. Uncover, add the peach slices and bake for a further 10 minutes before serving.
Serves 4
Total Calories 780
195 Calories per portion

Haddock au Gratin

METRIC/IMPERIAL	AMERICAN
100 g/4 oz haddock, poached in milk and drained	¼ lb haddock, poached in milk and drained
15 g/½ oz butter	1 tablespoon butter
25 g/1 oz button mushrooms, sliced	¼ cup button mushrooms, sliced
15 g/½ oz flour	2 tablespoons flour
7 tablespoons skimmed milk	7 tablespoons skim milk
25 g/1 oz low-fat hard cheese, grated	¼ cup low-fat hard cheese, grated
salt	salt
freshly ground black pepper	freshly ground black pepper
Topping:	**Topping:**
25 g/1 oz Bran Flakes, crushed	1 cup Bran Flakes, crushed
15 g/½ oz butter	1 tablespoon butter
To garnish:	**To garnish:**
tomato wedges	tomato wedges
1 tablespoon chopped fresh parsley	1 tablespoon chopped fresh parsley

Flake the fish, removing any skin and bones, and divide between four scallop shells or individual ovenproof dishes. Melt the butter in a saucepan and gently sauté the mushrooms until tender. Add the flour and cook for 1 minute. Remove from the heat and gradually stir in the milk. Return to the heat and bring to the boil, stirring all the time. Cook for 1 minute, then remove from the heat and add the cheese, and salt and pepper to taste. Stir until the cheese has melted, then pour the sauce over the fish.
To make the topping, place the Bran Flakes in a bowl and rub (cut) in the butter. Sprinkle the mixture over the sauce and bake in a preheated hot oven (220°C/425°F, Gas Mark 7) for about 15 minutes. Garnish with tomato wedges and chopped parsley.
Serves 2
Total Calories 585
293 Calories per portion

Gouda and Prawn (Shrimp) Moulds

METRIC/IMPERIAL	AMERICAN
225 g/8 oz peeled prawns, chopped	½ lb shelled shrimp, chopped
75 g/3 oz cooked long-grain rice	⅔ cup cooked long-grain rice
50 g/2 oz canned pimento	¼ cup canned pimiento
½ dessert apple, cored and chopped	½ dessert apple, cored and chopped
50 g/2 oz button mushrooms, chopped	½ cup button mushrooms, chopped
50 g/2 oz Gouda cheese, finely grated	½ cup finely grated Gouda cheese
2 tablespoons low-calorie mayonnaise	2 tablespoons low-calorie mayonnaise
½ teaspoon Tabasco sauce	½ teaspoon hot pepper sauce
salt	salt
freshly ground black pepper	freshly ground black pepper
lettuce to serve	lettuce to serve
To garnish:	**To garnish:**
small bunch watercress	small bunch watercress
strips of pimento	strips of pimiento

Mix together all the ingredients, except the lettuce, in a bowl and spoon into four individual ramekin dishes or eight dariole moulds. Press the mixture down well and chill in the refrigerator until set. To serve, turn out the moulds onto a bed of lettuce on a serving platter or on individual serving plates. Garnish with watercress and strips of pimento.
Serves 4
Total Calories 685
171 Calories per portion

Mediterranean Noodles

METRIC/IMPERIAL	AMERICAN
1 × 400 g/14 oz can tomatoes	1 × 14 oz can tomatoes
2 celery sticks, finely chopped	2 stalks celery, finely chopped
225 g/8 oz button mushrooms, sliced	2 cups button mushrooms, sliced
1 × 200 g/7 oz can tuna in brine, drained and roughly flaked	1 × 7 oz can tuna in brine, drained and roughly flaked
1 clove garlic, crushed	1 clove garlic, crushed
½ teaspoon dried mixed herbs or basil	½ teaspoon dried mixed herbs or basil
salt	salt
freshly ground black pepper	freshly ground black pepper
225 g/8 oz ribbon noodles	½ lb ribbon noodles

Place the tomatoes and celery in a saucepan and bring to the boil. Cover and simmer for 5 minutes. Add the mushrooms, tuna, garlic, herbs and salt and pepper to taste. Simmer for a further 10 minutes.

Meanwhile, cook the noodles in boiling salted water until just tender, or according to packet instructions. Drain well and serve with the tuna sauce.
Serves 4
Total Calories 1120 (using 225 g/8 oz (4 cups) ribbon noodles)
280 Calories per portion

Stuffed Trout

METRIC/IMPERIAL	AMERICAN
40 g/1½ oz All-Bran	¾ cup All-Bran
120 ml/4 fl oz skimmed milk	½ cup skim milk
15 g/½ oz margarine	1 tablespoon margarine
½ onion, finely chopped	½ onion, finely chopped
50 g/2 oz button mushrooms, finely chopped	½ cup finely chopped button mushrooms
½ teaspoon grated lemon rind	½ teaspoon grated lemon rind
½ teaspoon dried thyme	½ teaspoon dried thyme
salt	salt
freshly ground black pepper	freshly ground black pepper
2 trout, cleaned	2 trout, cleaned

Put the All-Bran and milk into a bowl and leave for 10 minutes until the milk has been absorbed. Melt the margarine in a saucepan, add the onion, mushrooms, lemon rind and thyme and cook gently for a few minutes. Cool, then add to the All-Bran with salt and pepper to taste.

Mix well, then stuff the fish with the mixture.

Wrap each fish loosely in foil and cook in a preheated moderately hot oven (190°C/375°F, Gas Mark 5) for about 30 minutes or until the fish is tender.
Serves 2
Total Calories 670
335 Calories per portion

Cod with Loganberry Sauce

METRIC/IMPERIAL	AMERICAN
4 cod steaks	4 cod steaks
salt	salt
freshly ground black pepper	freshly ground black pepper
120 ml/4 fl oz skimmed milk	½ cup skim milk
Sauce:	**Sauce:**
1 × 285 g/13½ oz can loganberries in natural juice	1 × 13½ oz can loganberries in natural juice
4 pickled cucumbers, diced	4 dill pickles, diced
2 teaspoons arrowroot	2 teaspoons arrowroot

Place the cod steaks in an ovenproof dish and sprinkle with salt and pepper. Pour over the milk, then cover and bake in a preheated moderate oven (180°C/350°F, Gas Mark 4) for 30 minutes.

Meanwhile, place the loganberries in a saucepan with the cucumbers (dill pickles) and heat gently. Mix the arrowroot with a little water to form a smooth paste, then add to the loganberry mixture, stirring well. Heat until the mixture thickens. Drain the cod and serve with the sauce.
Serves 4
Total Calories 640
160 Calories per portion

MAIN COURSES

Stuffed Breast of Veal

METRIC/IMPERIAL	AMERICAN
1 kg/2 lb breast of veal, boned	2 lb breast of veal, boned
4 eggs, beaten	4 eggs, beaten
salt	salt
freshly ground black pepper	freshly ground black pepper
4 slices lean ham	4 slices lean ham
1 to 2 teaspoons chopped fresh tarragon or ½ to 1 teaspoon dried tarragon	1 to 2 teaspoons chopped tarragon or ½ to 1 teaspoon dried tarragon

Unroll the veal and flatten out if necessary. Remove as much fat as possible.

Season the eggs with salt and pepper. Pour into a non-stick frying pan (skillet). As the omelette begins to set underneath, tilt the pan to let the liquid egg run to the side of the pan. The omelette is cooked when the centre is still creamy.

Place the open omelette on the veal. It will be necessary to trim the omelette and put the side pieces on top.

Lay the slices of ham over the omelette, again trimming to fit the veal. Sprinkle with the tarragon.

Roll up the veal and tie at intervals with string. Place in a roasting tin (pan).

Bake in a preheated moderately hot oven (200°C/400°F, Gas Mark 6) for 1½ hours, basting and turning frequently. Serve hot or cold.
Serves 4
Total Calories 2080
260 Calories per 100 g/4 oz (¼ lb) portion

Rosy Pears (page 52)
Stuffed Breast of Veal

Slimmers' Quiche

METRIC/IMPERIAL	AMERICAN
7 slices slimmers' bread	7 slices slimmers' bread
15 g/½ oz low-fat spread	1 tablespoon low-fat spread
50 g/2 oz Edam cheese, grated	½ cup grated Edam cheese
2 tomatoes, sliced	2 tomatoes, sliced
½ teaspoon dried marjoram	½ teaspoon dried marjoram
2 eggs, beaten	2 eggs, beaten
300 ml/½ pint skimmed milk	1¼ cups skim milk
salt	salt
freshly ground black pepper	freshly ground black pepper
3 anchovy fillets, slit lengthwise	3 anchovy fillets, slit lengthwise
6 black olives	6 ripe olives
15 g/½ oz grated Parmesan cheese to serve	1 tablespoon grated Parmesan cheese to serve

Spread the bread slices sparingly with the low-fat spread and arrange the slices, spread side down, around the base and sides of a 20 cm/8 inch flan tin (pie pan). Bake in a preheated moderately hot oven (200°C/400°F, Gas Mark 6) for 10 minutes, until crisp and pale golden brown.

Scatter the Edam cheese into the bread case (pie shell) and arrange the sliced tomatoes on top. Sprinkle with marjoram. Mix the eggs with the milk and salt and pepper to taste, then pour over the cheese and tomatoes. Return to the oven and bake for 15 minutes. Remove from the oven and arrange the anchovy strips and olives on top of the filling, then return to the oven for a further 10 to 15 minutes, until set.

Serve warm, sprinkled with Parmesan cheese.
Serves 4 to 6
Total Calories 805
201 to 134 Calories per portion

Lamb Parcels

METRIC/IMPERIAL	AMERICAN
4 lamb chops, trimmed of fat	4 lamb chops, trimmed of fat
½ teaspoon mustard	½ teaspoon mustard
1 teaspoon chopped fresh thyme	1 teaspoon chopped fresh thyme
few sprigs fresh mint to garnish	few sprigs fresh mint to garnish
Topping:	**Topping:**
25 g/1 oz low-fat spread	2 tablespoons low-fat spread
1 onion, sliced	1 onion, sliced
½ green pepper, cored, seeded and sliced	½ green pepper, cored, seeded and sliced
1 teaspoon vinegar	1 teaspoon vinegar
2 teaspoons soy sauce	2 teaspoons soy sauce
100 g/4 oz canned pineapple in natural juice, drained and chopped	4 oz canned pineapple in natural juice, drained and chopped
1 tablespoon flour	1 tablespoon flour
7 tablespoons stock	7 tablespoons stock
salt	salt
freshly ground black pepper	freshly ground black pepper

Place each chop on a piece of foil, spread with the mustard and sprinkle with the thyme. To make the topping, melt the low-fat spread in a saucepan and sauté the onion and pepper for 5 minutes, until soft. Add the remaining ingredients and bring to the boil, stirring. Cook for 2 to 3 minutes, then pile on top of each chop.

Fold over the foil to make a parcel, seal and bake in a preheated moderate oven (180°C/350°F, Gas Mark 4) for 1 hour. Remove the foil and serve the chops garnished with mint.

Serves 4
Total Calories 1100
275 Calories per portion

Breton Lamb

METRIC/IMPERIAL	AMERICAN
150 g/5 oz dried haricot beans, soaked overnight	⅔ cup dried navy beans, soaked overnight
1 onion	1 onion
salt	salt
freshly ground black pepper	freshly ground black pepper
1 bouquet garni	1 bouquet garni
1 × 1.5 kg/3 lb leg of lamb	1 × 3 lb leg of lamb
1 clove garlic, cut into slivers	1 clove garlic, cut into slivers
15 g/½ oz low-fat spread	1 tablespoon low-fat spread
1 small onion, chopped	1 small onion, chopped
2 large tomatoes, peeled and chopped	2 large tomatoes, peeled and chopped

Drain the beans and place in a large saucepan with the whole onion, salt, pepper and bouquet garni. Add enough fresh cold water to cover and bring slowly to the boil. Simmer gently for 1 hour or until the beans are tender.

Make diagonal slashes in the surface of the leg of lamb with a sharp knife and press in the slivers of garlic. Dust with salt and pepper and rub over with half the low-fat spread. Place on a rack in a roasting tin (pan) and cook in a preheated moderately hot oven (190°C/375°F, Gas Mark 5), allowing 20 minutes per 450 g (1 lb), plus 20 minutes.

Strain the beans and onion and keep warm. When the meat is cooked, remove to a serving dish and keep warm. Remove 1 tablespoon of juices from the roasting tin (pan) and reserve. Melt the remaining low-fat spread in a saucepan, add the chopped onion, tomatoes and boiled onion and simmer gently until softened, adding salt and pepper to taste. Add the reserved meat juices and the cooked beans and mix well. Pour over the meat and serve hot.

Serves 4
Total Calories 2415
604 Calories per portion

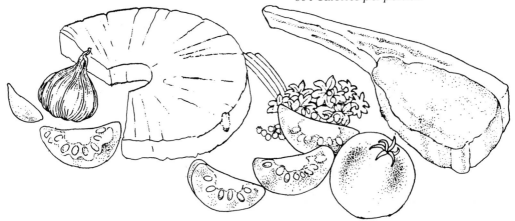

Lamb with Loganberry Mint Sauce

METRIC/IMPERIAL	AMERICAN
4 lamb chops, trimmed of fat	4 lamb chops, trimmed of fat
salt	salt
freshly ground black pepper	freshly ground black pepper
Sauce:	**Sauce:**
1 × 285 g/9½ oz can loganberries in natural juice	1 × 9½ oz can loganberries in natural juice
2 tablespoons chopped fresh mint	2 tablespoons chopped fresh mint
1 tablespoon concentrated mint sauce	1 tablespoon concentrated mint sauce
salt	salt
freshly ground black pepper	freshly ground black pepper

Season the chops with salt and pepper and grill (broil) for 8 to 9 minutes on each side, until brown.

To make the sauce, heat the loganberries in a small saucepan with the mint and mint sauce. Add salt and pepper to taste. Serve hot with the chops.
Serves 4
Total Calories 970
242 Calories per portion

Curried Chicken Hot-pot

METRIC/IMPERIAL	AMERICAN
4 chicken drumsticks	4 chicken drumsticks
1 large onion, sliced	1 large onion, sliced
2 carrots, diced	2 carrots, diced
2 large tomatoes, peeled and chopped	2 large tomatoes, peeled and chopped
225 g/8 oz apple, chopped	2 cups chopped apple
600 ml/1 pint boiling chicken stock	2½ cups boiling chicken stock
2 teaspoons curry paste	2 teaspoons curry paste
salt	salt
freshly ground black pepper	freshly ground black pepper
To serve:	**To serve:**
boiled rice	boiled rice
fresh pineapple	fresh pineapple
sliced tomato	sliced tomato
plain yogurt	plain yogurt
chopped cucumber	chopped cucumber

Place the chicken drumsticks in a small ovenproof casserole with the vegetables and apple. Add the stock, curry paste, salt and pepper.

Cover and cook in a preheated moderate oven (160°C/325°F, Gas Mark 3) for 1 hour. Serve with boiled rice and side dishes of fresh pineapple, sliced tomatoes and plain yogurt with chopped cucumber.
Serves 4
Total Calories 560 (without accompaniments)
140 Calories per portion (without accompaniments)

Celebration Chicken

METRIC/IMPERIAL	AMERICAN
225 g/8 oz low-fat soft cheese	1 cup low-fat soft cheese
1 tablespoon lemon juice	1 tablespoon lemon juice
1 tablespoon curry powder	1 tablespoon curry powder
salt	salt
freshly ground black pepper	freshly ground black pepper
450 g/1 lb cold cooked chicken, diced	1 lb cold cooked chicken, diced
350 g/12 oz cooked rice, coloured with saffron or turmeric	2 cups cooked rice, colored with saffron or turmeric
25 g/1 oz toasted desiccated coconut	⅓ cup toasted shredded coconut
To garnish:	**To garnish:**
few sprigs watercress	few sprigs watercress
lemon wedges	lemon wedges

Mix the cheese with the lemon juice, curry powder and salt and pepper to taste. Gently mix in the chicken.

Serve on a bed of cold coloured rice. Sprinkle with coconut and garnish with watercress and lemon wedges. This is also an excellent way to use up leftover turkey.
Serves 4
Total Calories 1500
375 Calories per portion

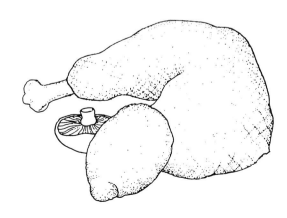

Boiled Chicken with Tarragon Rice

METRIC/IMPERIAL	AMERICAN
1 × 1.5 kg/3 lb boiling fowl	1 × 3 lb boiling fowl
1 large carrot, peeled	1 large carrot, peeled
1 small turnip, peeled	1 small turnip, peeled
1 large onion, peeled	1 large onion, peeled
1 bouquet garni	1 bouquet garni
salt	salt
freshly ground black pepper	freshly ground black pepper
Tarragon Rice:	**Tarragon Rice:**
100 g/4 oz long-grain rice	½ cup long-grain rice
salt	salt
1 red pepper, cored, seeded and sliced	1 red pepper, cored, seeded and sliced
1 tablespoon tarragon vinegar	1 tablespoon tarragon vinegar
1 tablespoon vegetable oil	1 tablespoon vegetable oil
freshly ground black pepper	freshly ground black pepper
2 teaspoons chopped fresh tarragon or 1 teaspoon dried tarragon	2 teaspoons chopped fresh or 1 teaspoon dried tarragon

Put the boiling fowl in a large saucepan with the whole carrot, turnip and onion. Add the bouquet garni, salt and pepper. Cover with water and bring to the boil. Cover and simmer for about 2 hours (depending on the age of the bird), skimming the water occasionally.

Put the rice in a saucepan of boiling salted water and simmer for 12 to 15 minutes or until cooked but still slightly firm.

Blanch the pepper in boiling water for 1 minute. Drain the rice and add the red pepper.

Stir in the tarragon vinegar, oil and salt and pepper to taste. Spoon into a heated serving dish and sprinkle with the chopped tarragon.

Remove the bird from the pan, remove the skin and carve the meat.

Serve the chicken with the rice. Also delicious served cold.
Serves 4
300 Calories per 100 g/4 oz (¼ lb) portion with 75 g/3 oz (⅓ cup) rice.

Chicken with Prune and Apple Stuffing

METRIC/IMPERIAL	AMERICAN
1 × 1.5 kg/3 lb chicken	1 × 3 lb chicken
Stuffing:	**Stuffing:**
175 g/6 oz fresh breadcrumbs	1½ cups fresh bread crumbs
12 prunes, soaked overnight and chopped	12 prunes, soaked overnight and chopped
2 large apples, cored and cut into chunks	2 large apples, cored and cut into chunks
grated rind and juice of 1 lemon	grated rind and juice of 1 lemon
1 egg, beaten	1 egg, beaten
skimmed milk, if necessary	skim milk, if necessary
salt	salt
freshly ground black pepper	freshly ground black pepper

For the stuffing, mix together the breadcrumbs, prunes, apple and lemon rind. Add the beaten egg and lemon juice to bind. If necessary, stir in a little milk. Add salt and pepper to taste.

Spoon the stuffing into the body cavity of the bird.

Place the chicken in a roasting tin half filled with water and roast for about 1½ hours in a preheated moderately hot oven (200°C/400°F, Gas Mark 6) for about 1½ hours.
Serves 4
375 Calories per portion (75 g/3 oz chicken meat without skin with 1 heaped dessert spoon stuffing)

Chicken with Prune and Apple Stuffing
Boiled Chicken with Tarragon Rice
Citrus Chicken (page 32)

Tasty Meat Loaf

METRIC/IMPERIAL	AMERICAN
450 g/1 lb lean beef, minced	1 lb lean beef, ground
1 small onion, finely chopped	1 small onion, finely chopped
50 g/2 oz low-calorie breadcrumbs	1 cup low-calorie bread crumbs
1 tablespoon chopped fresh parsley	1 tablespoon chopped fresh parsley
1 × 175 g/6 oz can tomatoes, sieved	1 × 6 oz can tomatoes, sieved
1 egg, beaten	1 egg, beaten
2 teaspoons Worcestershire sauce	2 teaspoons Worcestershire sauce
½ teaspoon salt	½ teaspoon salt
freshly ground black pepper	freshly ground black pepper
To garnish:	**To garnish:**
lettuce leaves	lettuce leaves
tomato slices	tomato slices

Mix all the ingredients thoroughly together and pack tightly into a lightly oiled 1 kg/2 lb loaf tin (9 × 5 inch loaf pan). Cover with foil and bake on the centre shelf of a preheated moderate oven (180°C/350°F, Gas Mark 4) for 1½ hours.

Turn out and serve hot or cold garnished with lettuce and tomato.
Serves 4 to 5
Total Calories 975
244 to 195 Calories per portion

Cidered Beef Casserole

METRIC/IMPERIAL	AMERICAN
25 g/1 oz low-fat spread	2 tablespoons low-fat spread
1 onion, sliced	1 onion, sliced
3 celery sticks, sliced	3 stalks celery, sliced
1 clove garlic, crushed	1 clove garlic, crushed
300 ml/½ pint dry cider	1¼ cups hard cider
3 tablespoons cider vinegar	3 tablespoons cider vinegar
salt	salt
freshly ground black pepper	freshly ground black pepper
450 g/1 lb braising steak, cubed	1 lb braising steak, cubed
150 ml/¼ pint boiling beef stock	⅔ cup boiling beef stock
12 black olives, stoned	12 pitted ripe olives
100 g/4 oz button mushrooms, quartered	1 cup button mushrooms, quartered

Melt the low-fat spread in a saucepan and sauté the onion, celery and garlic until beginning to brown. Add

the cider, vinegar and salt and pepper to taste and bring to the boil. Simmer for 5 mnutes then pour ove the steak and leave to marinate for 2 to 3 hours.

Transfer the meat and marinade to an ovenproo casserole, then add the stock, olives and mushrooms Cover and cook in a preheated moderate over (180°C/350°F, Gas Mark 4) for 1½ to 2 hours, until th meat is tender.
Serves 4
Total Calories 1010
252 Calories per portion

Beef with Ginger and Almonds

METRIC/IMPERIAL	AMERICAN
½ tablespoon vegetable oil	½ tablespoon vegetable oil
50 g/2 oz almonds, blanched	½ cup almonds, blanched
350 g/12 oz lean beef, cut into thin strips	¾ lb lean beef, cut into thin strips
100 g/4 oz button mushrooms, chopped	1 cup button mushrooms, chopped
25 g/1 oz stem ginger, finely sliced	1 tablespoon finely sliced preserved ginger
2 tablespoons cornflour	2 tablespoons cornstarch
120 ml/4 fl oz beef stock	½ cup beef stock
1 tablespoon soy sauce	1 tablespoon soy sauce
salt	salt
freshly ground black pepper	freshly ground black pepper
225 g/8 oz boiled rice to serve	1⅓ cups boiled rice to serve

Heat the oil in a non-stick frying pan (skillet) and fry the almonds, beef, mushrooms and ginger for about 5 minutes. Remove from the pan and keep hot. Blend the cornflour (cornstarch) with the stock and soy sauce and stir into the juices in the pan. Heat gently, stirring all the time, until the sauce thickens. Return the mea mixture to the pan and add salt and pepper to taste Simmer for a few minutes, then serve immediately with boiled rice.
Serves 2
Total Calories 1385
692 Calories per portion

Sweet and Sour Pork

METRIC/IMPERIAL	AMERICAN
4 teaspoons butter	4 teaspoons butter
2 cloves garlic, crushed	2 cloves garlic, crushed
450 g/1 lb cooked pork, diced	1 lb cooked pork, diced
2 carrots, cut into 1 cm/ ½ inch slices	2 carrots, cut into ½ inch slices
½ cucumber, cut lengthwise into thin strips	½ cucumber, cut lengthwise into thin strips
1 onion, cut into wedges	1 onion, cut into wedges
1 × 440 g/15½ oz can pineapple rings in natural juice	1 × 15½ oz can pineapple rings in natural juice
2 teaspoons cornflour	2 teaspoons cornstarch
3 tablespoons soy sauce	3 tablespoons soy sauce
3 tablespoons vinegar	3 tablespoons vinegar

Melt the butter in a saucepan and sauté the garlic for 5 minutes. Add the pork, carrots, cucumber and onion. Roughly chop the pineapple, reserving the juice.

Add the pineapple to the pan and cook together for 20 minutes. Blend the cornflour with the reserved pineapple juice, soy sauce and vinegar. Add to the pork and cook for 2 to 3 minutes more before serving. Serve with plain boiled rice and stir-fried vegetables.
Serves 4
Total Calories 1430
358 Calories per portion

Pork Kebabs with Barbecue Sauce

METRIC/IMPERIAL	AMERICAN
450 g/1 lb lean pork, diced	1 lb lean pork, diced
2 small onions, quartered	2 small onions, quartered
100 g/4 oz button mushrooms	1 cup button mushrooms
4 bay leaves	4 bay leaves
1 tablespoon vegetable oil	1 tablespoon vegetable oil
boiled rice to serve	boiled rice to serve
Sauce:	**Sauce:**
1 tablespoon low-fat spread	1 tablespoon low-fat spread
1 clove garlic, crushed	1 clove garlic, crushed
100 g/4 oz tomato purée	½ cup tomato paste
2 tablespoons wine vinegar	2 tablespoons wine vinegar
2 tablespoons soy sauce	2 tablespoons soy sauce
3 tablespoons lemon juice	3 tablespoons lemon juice
2 tablespoons Worcestershire sauce	2 tablespoons Worcestershire sauce
10 drops liquid sweetener	10 drops liquid sweetener

Thread the pork, onions, mushrooms and bay leaves alternately on to four skewers. Brush lightly with oil, then grill (broil) for 10 to 15 minutes, until cooked.

Meanwhile, to make the sauce, gently melt the low-fat spread in a saucepan and add the garlic. Sauté for a few minutes, then add the remaining ingredients. Bring to the boil, stirring continuously. Serve the kebabs hot on a bed of rice with the sauce.
Serves 4
Total Calories 1020 (without rice)
255 Calories per portion (without rice)

Spinach Cottage Pancakes (Crêpes)

METRIC/IMPERIAL	AMERICAN
Pancakes:	**Pancakes:**
100 g/4 oz plain flour	1 cup all-purpose flour
pinch of salt	pinch of salt
1 egg	1 egg
300 ml/½ pint skimmed milk	1¼ cups skim milk
15 g/½ oz low-fat spread	1 tablespoon low-fat spread
Filling and Topping:	**Filling and Topping:**
225 g/8 oz cottage cheese	1 cup cottage cheese
150 ml/¼ pint plain yogurt	⅔ cup plain yogurt
1 egg	1 egg
salt	salt
freshly ground black pepper	freshly ground black pepper
225 g/8 oz frozen spinach, thawed and thoroughly drained	1 cup frozen spinach, thawed and thoroughly drained
25 g/1 oz flaked almonds	¼ cup slivered almonds

To make the pancake (crêpe) batter, combine the flour and salt in a mixing bowl and make a well in the centre. Add the egg and whisk, gradually adding half the milk and incorporating the flour, until smooth. Mix in the remaining milk. Alternatively, the batter may be mixed in a blender or food processor.

Heat a little low-fat spread in a non-stick frying pan (skillet), then add just enough batter to cover the bottom of the pan. Fry quickly, turning once, until golden brown. Remove from the pan and keep warm. Repeat to make eight pancakes (crêpes).

To make the filling and topping, blend the cottage cheese, yogurt, egg, salt and pepper in a blender or food processor until smooth. Alternatively, beat together thoroughly in a bowl. Divide this mixture in half and add the spinach to one half. Divide the spinach mixture between the pancakes (crêpes), roll up and place in a shallow ovenproof dish. Pour over the remaining cottage cheese mixture and sprinkle with the almonds. Bake in a preheated moderately hot oven (190°C/375°F, Gas Mark 5) for 20 minutes.
Serves 4
Total Calories 1230
307 Calories per portion

Beef Stroganoff

METRIC/IMPERIAL	AMERICAN
150 ml/¼ pint plain yogurt	⅔ cup plain yogurt
1 teaspoon Dijon mustard	1 teaspoon Dijon-style mustard
salt	salt
freshly ground black pepper	freshly ground black pepper
2 large onions, peeled and chopped	2 large onions, peeled and chopped
about 150 ml/¼ pint beef stock	about ⅔ cup beef stock
2 tablespoons dry sherry	2 tablespoons dry sherry
450 g/1 lb beef fillet or sirloin steak, cut into wafer-thin strips	1 lb beef fillet or sirloin steak, cut into wafer-thin strips
100 g/4 oz mushrooms, sliced	1 cup sliced mushrooms

Mix the yogurt, mustard, salt and pepper together and set aside.

Put the onions in a saucepan with just enough stock to cover the bottom of the pan. Add the sherry. Cook the onions over a low heat for about 10 minutes until soft, adding more stock if necessary. When the onions are clear, add the beef and mushrooms and increase the heat.

Cook for 1 minute, stirring rapidly.

Remove from the heat and stir in the yogurt mixture. Serve immediately.

Serves 4
Total Calories 1200
300 Calories per portion

Herb Stuffed Sirloin

METRIC/IMPERIAL	AMERICAN
750 g/1½ lb sirloin steak, in one piece	1½ lb sirloin steak, in one piece
2 slices bread	2 slices bread
50 g/2 oz grated Parmesan cheese	½ cup grated Parmesan cheese
2 teaspoons chopped fresh mixed herbs or 1 teaspoon dried mixed herbs	2 teaspoons chopped fresh mixed herbs or 1 teaspoon dried mixed herbs
50 g/2 oz finely chopped onion	½ cup finely chopped onion
salt	salt
freshly ground black pepper	freshly ground black pepper
1 tablespoon Worcestershire sauce	1 tablespoon Worcestershire sauce

Beat the steak into a thin strip using a meat mallet o rolling pin.

Dip the bread into cold water, squeeze the water ou then break into small pieces. Mix with the cheese herbs, onion and salt and pepper to taste.

Sprinkle Worcestershire sauce and salt over th steak. Spoon the stuffing onto the steak and spread Roll up and tie firmly.

Wrap the beef roll in foil and cook in a preheate moderately hot oven (190°C/375°F, Gas Mark 5) fo about 1 hour.

Serve hot or cold.

Serves 4
230 Calories per 100 g/4 oz portion

Kidney and Mushroom Casserole

METRIC/IMPERIAL	AMERICAN
450 g/1 lb lamb's kidneys, skinned and cored	1 lb lamb's kidneys, skinned and cored
100 g/4 oz onions, peeled and chopped	1 cup chopped onions
300 ml/½ pint beef stock	1¼ cups beef stock
120 ml/4 fl oz sherry	½ cup sherry
salt	salt
freshly ground black pepper	freshly ground black pepper
225 g/8 oz mushrooms, stalks removed, sliced if large	½ lb mushrooms, stalks removed, sliced if large

Halve or slice the kidneys. Place under a preheated h grill and cook for 1 minute on each side.

Transfer to an ovenproof casserole dish and add th onions, stock, sherry and salt and pepper to taste. Sti in the mushrooms.

Cover and cook in a preheated moderately hot over (200°C/400°F, Gas Mark 6) for about 40 minutes or unti the kidneys are tender. Serve with plain boiled rice.

Serves 4
230 Calories per 100 g/4 oz portion

Beef Stroganof
Kidney and Mushroom Casserole
(Photograph: Mushroom Grower's Association)

30

Citrus Chicken

METRIC/IMPERIAL	AMERICAN
1 × 1.5 kg/3 lb chicken	1 × 3 lb chicken
2 small turnips, peeled	2 small turnips, peeled
2 carrots, peeled	2 carrots, peeled
100 g/4 oz onion, peeled and chopped	1 cup chopped onion
grated rind of 1 lemon	grated rind of 1 lemon
salt	salt
freshly ground black pepper	freshly ground black pepper
2 tablespoons lemon juice	2 tablespoons lemon juice
1 large wine glass wine vinegar	1 large wine glass wine vinegar
liquid sweetener (optional)	liquid sweetener (optional)
1 tablespoon cornflour	1 tablespoon cornstarch
orange slices, to garnish	orange slices, to garnish

Place the chicken in a large saucepan with the vegetables, lemon rind and salt and pepper to taste.

Cover with water and bring to the boil. Cover and simmer gently for about 2 hours, skimming occasionally.

When the chicken is cooked, remove from the pan. Spoon 300 ml/½ pint (1¼ cups) stock into a saucepan. Add the lemon juice, wine vinegar and sweetener, if using. Simmer for 4 minutes.

Blend the cornflour (cornstarch) with a little of the remaining stock. Add to the mixture and cook for 3 minutes until fairly thick and almost transparent.

Carve the chicken and place the slices on a heated serving dish. Pour over the sauce and leave to cool. Garnish with orange slices. Serve with the vegetables cooked with the chicken or with a green salad.
Serves 4
Total Calories 1070
265 Calories per 75 g/3 oz portion

Stuffed Chicken Breasts

METRIC/IMPERIAL	AMERICAN
50 g/2 oz low-fat spread	¼ cup low-fat spread
1 clove garlic, crushed (optional)	1 clove garlic, crushed (optional)
1 tablespoon chopped fresh parsley	1 tablespoon chopped fresh parsley
1 tablespoon chopped fresh marjoram or thyme	1 tablespoon chopped fresh marjoram or thyme
salt	salt
freshly ground black pepper	freshly ground black pepper
4 chicken breasts, skinned	4 chicken breasts, skinned
100 g/4 oz smoked salmon (optional)	¼ lb smoked salmon (optional)
2 tablespoons lemon juice	2 tablespoons lemon juice

Mix the low-fat spread, garlic (if using), herbs and salt and pepper to taste. Make a slit three-quarters of the way through each chicken breast and spread inside with the herb mixture. Divide the salmon (if using) into four and tuck into the pockets cut in the chicken. Place in an ovenproof dish and sprinkle with lemon juice. Cover with foil and bake in a preheated moderately hot oven (190°C/375°F, Gas Mark 5) for 30 minutes. Serve hot or cold with vegetables or salad.
Serves 4
Total Calories 1030 (without salmon); 1190 (with salmon)
257 Calories per portion (without salmon)
297 Calories per portion (with salmon)

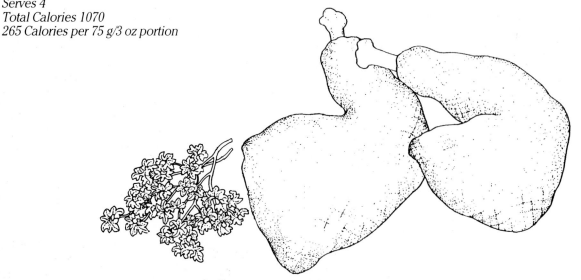

Liver with Raspberries

METRIC/IMPERIAL	AMERICAN
4 teaspoons margarine	4 teaspoons margarine
1 small onion, finely chopped	1 small onion, finely chopped
1 large clove garlic, crushed (optional)	1 large clove garlic, crushed (optional)
450 g/1 lb calves' or lambs' liver, thinly sliced	1 lb calves' or lambs' liver, thinly sliced
3 tablespoons chopped fresh sage	3 tablespoons chopped fresh sage
1 × 300 g/10 oz can raspberries in natural juice	1 × 10 oz can raspberries in natural juice
salt	salt
freshly ground black pepper	freshly ground black pepper
1 tablespoon lemon juice	1 tablespoon lemon juice

Melt the margarine in a pan and sauté the onion and garlic (if using) for 5 minutes, until soft. Add the liver and cook for a further 5 minutes, turning once, until brown. Remove from the pan, arrange on a serving dish and keep warm.

Add the sage, raspberry juice, salt, pepper and lemon juice to the pan and cook over a high heat until the sauce thickens. Add the raspberries and serve spooned over the liver.

Serves 4
Total Calories 1100
275 Calories per portion

Chilli Con Carne

METRIC/IMPERIAL	AMERICAN
450 g/1 lb minced beef	1 lb ground beef
1 small onion, sliced	½ cup sliced onions
1 clove garlic, peeled and crushed	1 clove garlic, peeled and crushed
1-3 teaspoons chilli powder (according to taste)	1-3 teaspoons chili powder (according to taste)
2 tablespoons tomato purée	2 tablespoons tomato paste
300 ml/½ pint water	1¼ cups water
1 × 439 g/15½ oz can red kidney beans, drained	1 × 15½ oz can red kidney beans, drained
salt	salt
freshly ground black pepper	freshly ground black pepper

Place the beef, onion, garlic, chilli powder (according to taste), tomato purée (paste) and water in a casserole and bring to the boil.

Cover and simmer gently for about 1¼ hours,
skimming the surface occasionally.

Add the beans and salt and pepper to taste. Simmer for a further 10 minutes. Serve immediately with a green salad.

Serves 4
Total Calories 1200
305 Calories per portion

Country Style Cannelloni

METRIC/IMPERIAL	AMERICAN
1 onion, finely chopped	1 onion, finely chopped
1 celery stick, finely chopped	1 stalk celery, finely chopped
1 carrot, finely chopped	1 carrot, finely chopped
150 g/5 oz cauliflower, finely chopped	1 cup finely chopped cauliflower
3 tablespoons tomato purée	3 tablespoons tomato paste
1 tablespoon chopped fresh parsley	1 tablespoon chopped fresh parsley
salt	salt
freshly ground black pepper	freshly ground black pepper
8 cannelloni tubes	8 cannelloni tubes
Cheese sauce:	**Cheese sauce:**
4 tablespoons cornflour	4 tablespoons cornstarch
600 ml/1 pint skimmed milk	2½ cups skim milk
salt	salt
freshly ground black pepper	freshly ground black pepper
100 g/4 oz low-fat cheese, grated	1 cup grated low-fat cheese

Mix the onion, celery, carrot and cauliflower in a bowl. Stir in the tomato purée (paste) and parsley and add salt and pepper to taste. Fill each cannelloni with the vegetable stuffing and set aside.

To make the sauce, blend the cornflour (cornstarch) with a little of the milk to form a smooth thin paste. Heat the remaining milk gently, stirring in the cornflour (cornstarch) paste. Bring to the boil, stirring, and simmer for 2 to 3 minutes, until thickened. Add salt and pepper to taste, then add half the cheese. Place 3 tablespoons of the sauce in the bottom of a shallow ovenproof dish. Arrange the cannelloni in a single layer on top, then pour over the remaining cheese sauce.

Sprinkle over the remaining cheese and bake in a preheated moderate oven (180°C/350°F, Gas Mark 4) for 45 to 50 minutes, until golden brown. Serve hot with a green salad.

Serves 4
Total Calories 1570
392 Calories per portion

VEGETABLES AND SALADS

Leeks with Orange and Thyme

METRIC/IMPERIAL	AMERICAN
3 slices lean bacon, chopped	3 slices lean bacon, chopped
500 g/1¼ lb leeks, trimmed and sliced	1¼ lb leeks, trimmed and sliced
grated rind and juice of 1 orange	grated rind and juice of 1 orange
1 tablespoon fresh thyme leaves or 1 teaspoon dried thyme	1 tablespoon fresh thyme leaves or 1 teaspoon dried thyme
salt	salt
freshly ground black pepper	freshly ground black pepper

Gently heat the bacon in a frying pan (skillet) until the fat begins to run. Add the leeks and fry for 2 minutes, stirring.

Make up the orange rind and juice to 150 ml/¼ pint (⅔ cup) with water, and add to the pan with the thyme, salt and pepper.

Bring to the boil and simmer for 10 to 15 minutes, stirring occasionally until the leeks are just tender and most of the juice has evaporated.

Serve hot or cold.
Serves 4
Total Calories 575
144 Calories per portion

Courgettes (Zucchini) Niçoise

METRIC/IMPERIAL	AMERICAN
2 tablespoons low-fat spread	2 tablespoons low-fat spread
1 onion, chopped	1 onion, chopped
1 clove garlic, crushed (optional)	1 clove garlic, crushed (optional)
450 g/1 lb courgettes, sliced	1 lb zucchini, sliced
225 g/8 oz tomatoes, peeled and sliced	½ lb tomatoes, peeled and sliced
salt	salt
freshly ground black pepper	freshly ground black pepper
1 tablespoon chopped fresh parsley to garnish	1 tablespoon chopped fresh parsley to garnish

Melt the spread in a frying pan (skillet) and fry the onion, garlic (if using) and courgettes (zucchini) for 5 minutes, or until lightly browned, turning occasionally. Stir in the tomatoes, salt and pepper.

Cover the pan and cook gently for 5 to 10 minutes, stirring occasionally until the tomatoes are reduced to a pulp and the courgettes (zucchini) are just tender.

Turn into a serving dish and sprinkle with parsley.
Serves 4
Total Calories 205
51 Calories per portion

Leeks with Orange and Thyme
Courgettes (Zucchini) Niçoise

Spiced Tomato Eggs

METRIC/IMPERIAL	AMERICAN
1 medium onion, grated	1 medium onion, grated
1 × 500 g/16 oz can tomatoes	1 × 16 oz can tomatoes
2 sweetener tablets, crushed	2 sweetener tablets, crushed
1 teaspoon Worcestershire sauce	1 teaspoon Worcestershire sauce
1 teaspoon finely grated orange rind	1 teaspoon finely grated orange rind
salt	salt
freshly ground black pepper	freshly ground black pepper
8 hard-boiled eggs	8 hard-cooked eggs
450 g/1 lb cauliflower florets	1 lb cauliflower flowerets
1 tablespoon chopped fresh parsley to garnish	1 tablespoon chopped fresh parsley to garnish

Put all the ingredients, except the eggs, cauliflower and parsley, into a saucepan. Simmer for about 10 minutes, mashing the tomatoes well to make a smooth sauce.

Cook the cauliflower in boiling salted water for 5 to 10 minutes, until just tender. Drain and arrange in a serving dish. Halve the eggs and place on top of the cauliflower. Pour the hot sauce over the top and serve immediately, sprinkled with chopped parsley.
Serves 4
Total Calories 795
199 Calories per portion

Aubergine (Eggplant) Eggs

METRIC/IMPERIAL	AMERICAN
4 aubergines	4 eggplants
2 tablespoons lemon juice	2 tablespoons lemon juice
225 g/8 oz button mushrooms	2 cups button mushrooms
8 hard-boiled eggs, chopped	8 hard-cooked eggs, chopped
salt	salt
freshly ground black pepper	freshly ground black pepper
1 × 150 g/5 oz carton plain yogurt	1 × 5 oz carton plain yogurt
pinch of paprika	pinch of paprika

Cut the aubergines (eggplants) in half lengthwise and score the flesh with a pointed knife. Sprinkle with lemon juice and cover the cut sides with foil. Wrap the mushrooms in foil and bake with the aubergines (eggplants) in a preheated moderately hot oven (200°C/400°F, Gas Mark 6) for about 20 minutes, until the aubergines (eggplants) are soft.

Scoop the flesh out of the aubergine (eggplant) halves, reserving the skins. Mash the flesh, then mix in the mushrooms, eggs, and salt and pepper to taste. Pile the mixture back into the skins, then spoon yogurt along the centre of each. Cover with foil and return to the oven for about 15 minutes to heat through. Sprinkle with paprika before serving hot with a green salad.
Serves 8
Total Calories 860
108 Calories per portion

Spicy Bran and Vegetable Salad

METRIC/IMPERIAL	AMERICAN
1 cauliflower, broken into florets	1 cauliflower, broken into flowerets
25 g/1 oz All-Bran	1 cup All-Bran
¼ teaspoon chilli powder	¼ teaspoon chili powder
¼ teaspoon dry mustard	¼ teaspoon dry mustard
pinch of garlic salt	pinch of garlic salt
25 g/1 oz low-fat spread, melted	2 tablespoons low-fat spread, melted
1 × 225 g/8 oz packet frozen French beans, cooked and drained	1 × 8 oz packet frozen whole green beans, cooked and drained
1 small onion, finely chopped	1 small onion, finely chopped

Blanch the cauliflower florets in boiling salted water for 5 minutes, then drain well and leave to cool. Mix together the All-Bran, chilli powder, mustard and garlic salt. Pour over the low-fat spread and stir well. Spread on an ovenproof plate and bake in a preheated moderately hot oven (200°C/400°F, Gas Mark 6) for 10 minutes.

Meanwhile, mix the cauliflower, beans and onion together in a serving bowl. Stir in the savoury bran mixture and serve. If liked, this salad may be tossed in a low-calorie dressing before serving.
Serves 4
Total Calories 320
80 Calories per portion

Hawaiian Salad

METRIC/IMPERIAL	AMERICAN
1 lettuce	1 lettuce
2 kiwifruit	2 kiwifruit
4 tomatoes, cut into wedges	4 tomatoes, cut into wedges
50 g/2 oz cucumber, sliced	½ cup sliced cucumber
6-8 radishes, trimmed	6-8 radishes, trimmed
1 orange, peeled and segmented	1 orange, peeled and segmented
50 g/2 oz celery, chopped	½ cup chopped celery
4 tablespoons low-calorie dressing	4 tablespoons low-calorie dressing

Line a serving plate with lettuce leaves. Peel and slice one kiwifruit and place in a bowl. Add all the remaining ingredients, except the reserved kiwifruit and dressing, and mix well. Pour over the dressing and toss well. Spoon on to the bed of lettuce. Peel and slice the remaining kiwifruit and use to garnish the salad.
Serves 4
Total Calories 200
50 Calories per portion

Mushroom and Apple Salad

METRIC/IMPERIAL	AMERICAN
2 dessert apples, cored, peeled and chopped	2 dessert apples, cored, peeled and chopped
1 tablespoon lemon juice	1 tablespoon lemon juice
225 g/8 oz button mushrooms, sliced	2 cups button mushrooms, sliced
50 g/2 oz cooked sweetcorn	½ cup cooked whole kernel corn
50 g/2 oz cucumber, peeled and diced	½ cup peeled and diced cucumber
100 g/4 oz celery, chopped	1 cup chopped celery
25 g/1 oz raisins	3 tablespoons raisins
150 ml/¼ pint low-calorie mayonnaise	⅔ cup low-calorie mayonnaise
1 cos lettuce	1 romaine lettuce

Put the apples in a bowl and sprinkle with the lemon juice to prevent them going brown. Add all the remaining ingredients, except the mayonnaise and lettuce, and mix carefully. Add the mayonnaise and mix again. Line a salad bowl with lettuce leaves and spoon the salad into the centre.
Serves 4
Total Calories 705
176 Calories per portion

Fennel and Orange Salad

METRIC/IMPERIAL	AMERICAN
1 lettuce	1 lettuce
1 large head fennel, trimmed and chopped	1 large head fennel, trimmed and chopped
3 oranges, peeled and segmented	3 oranges, peeled and segmented
1 bunch spring onions, chopped	1 bunch scallions, chopped
4 tablespoons low-calorie dressing	4 tablespoons low-calorie dressing
1 teaspoon French mustard	1 teaspoon Dijon-style mustard
salt	salt
freshly ground black pepper	freshly ground black pepper
50 g/2 oz Emmenthal cheese, cut into strips, to garnish	⅓ cup Emmenthal cheese strips to garnish

Tear the lettuce leaves into pieces and combine with the fennel, oranges and onions in a salad bowl. Mix the dressing with the mustard, and salt and pepper to taste, then pour over the salad. Toss until evenly covered and garnish with strips of cheese.
Serves 4
Total Calories 500
125 Calories per portion

Sweet and Sour Chinese Leaves

METRIC/IMPERIAL	AMERICAN
½ teaspoon salt	½ teaspoon salt
2 teaspoons sugar	2 teaspoons sugar
2 tablespoons wine vinegar	2 tablespoons wine vinegar
1 tablespoon soy sauce	1 tablespoon soy sauce
1 tablespoon vegetable oil	1 tablespoon vegetable oil
450 g/1 lb Chinese leaves, sliced	1 lb Chinese leaves, sliced

Mix together the salt, sugar, vinegar and soy sauce in a small bowl. Heat the oil in a large frying pan (skillet) or wok, add the Chinese leaves and cook quickly, stirring well. Add the vinegar mixture, cook for a few minutes more, then serve immediately.
Serves 4
Total Calories 215
54 Calories per portion

Dream Salad

METRIC/IMPERIAL	AMERICAN
½ canteloup or honeydew melon	½ canteloup or honeydew melon
100 g/4 oz carrots, grated	½ cup grated carrots
100 g/4 oz Edam cheese, cut into matchsticks	¼ lb Edam cheese, cut into matchsticks
¼ cucumber, diced	¼ cucumber, diced
100 g/4 oz strawberries, hulled and sliced	1 cup strawberries, hulled and sliced
2-3 tablespoons lemon juice	2-3 tablespoons lemon juice

Scoop the flesh out of the melon half, using a melon baller, or use a spoon and roughly chop the flesh. Place in the centre of a large flat serving dish. Arrange the carrots, cheese and cucumber in circles around the melon. Finish with a circle of strawberries around the edge of the plate. Sprinkle with lemon juice.
Serves 4
Total Calories 480
120 Calories per portion

Fennel with Tomatoes and Dill

METRIC/IMPERIAL	AMERICAN
4 small heads fennel	4 small roots fennel
little vegetable oil for frying	little vegetable oil for frying
salt	salt
freshly ground black pepper	freshly ground black pepper
450 g/1 lb tomatoes	1 lb tomatoes
3 tablespoons chopped dill	3 tablespoons chopped dill

Cut the fennel into very thin vertical slices. Brush the bottom of a non-stick pan with a little oil and stew the fennel gently, stirring often, until almost soft. Add plenty of salt and pepper. Skin and slice the tomatoes. Add them to the fennel and continue cooking gently for 5 minutes, stirring very carefully, now and again, to avoid breaking up the tomatoes. When ready, stir in the chopped dill and transfer to a dish to cool. Serve cold, but do not chill.
Serves 4
Total Calories 125
31 Calories per portion

Lettuce, Orange and Almond Salad

METRIC/IMPERIAL	AMERICAN
1 cos lettuce	1 romaine lettuce
1 bunch watercress	1 bunch watercress
3 small oranges, peeled and sliced	3 small oranges, peeled and sliced
25 g/1 oz flaked almonds	¼ cup slivered almonds
pinch of sugar	pinch of sugar
1 tablespoon chopped shallot	1 tablespoon chopped shallot
salt	salt
freshly ground black pepper	freshly ground black pepper
1 tablespoon orange juice	1 tablespoon orange juice
1 tablespoon lemon juice	1 tablespoon lemon juice
2 tablespoons olive oil	2 tablespoons olive oil

Tear the lettuce leaves into pieces and combine with sprigs of watercress in a salad bowl. Lay the orange slices over the salad and scatter with the almonds. Put the sugar and chopped shallot and salt and pepper to taste into a small bowl. Add the fruit juices and the oil and whisk to combine well. Pour over the salad just before serving.
Serves 4
Total Calories 560
140 Calories per portion

Red Cabbage and Apple Salad

METRIC/IMPERIAL	AMERICAN
225 g/8 oz red cabbage, finely shredded	3 cups finely shredded red cabbage
1 dessert apple, cored and chopped	1 dessert apple, cored and chopped
100 g/4 oz celery, chopped	1 cup chopped celery
1 onion, chopped	1 onion, chopped
Dressing:	**Dressing:**
100 g/4 oz low-fat soft cheese	½ cup low-fat soft cheese
1 tablespoon skimmed milk	1 tablespoon skim milk
salt	salt
freshly ground black pepper	freshly ground black pepper

Mix the cabbage, apple, celery and onion together in a salad bowl. Blend the dressing ingredients together, then pour over the salad and toss well. Cover and chill in the refrigerator before serving.
Serves 2 to 4
Total Calories 230
115 to 58 Calories per portion

Fennel with Tomatoes and Dill

Pommes Boulangères

METRIC/IMPERIAL	AMERICAN
750 g/1½ lb potatoes, thinly sliced	1½ lb potatoes, thinly sliced
1 large onion, thinly sliced	1 large onion, thinly sliced
150 ml/¼ pint skimmed milk	⅔ cup skim milk
100 g/4 oz low-fat soft cheese	½ cup low-fat soft cheese
salt	salt
freshly ground black pepper	freshly ground black pepper
1 clove garlic, crushed (optional)	1 clove garlic, crushed (optional)

Arrange the potatoes and onion in layers in a shallow ovenproof dish, overlapping the potatoes attractively on the top layer. Mix the milk gradually into the cheese and season well with salt, pepper and garlic (if using). Pour evenly over the potatoes, then bake in a preheated moderate oven (180°C/350°F, Gas Mark 4) for 1 hour, until pale golden brown and crispy.
Serves 4
Total Calories 720
180 Calories per portion

Cucumber and Fennel Salad

METRIC/IMPERIAL	AMERICAN
1 large cucumber	1 large cucumber
100 g/4 oz fennel	¼ lb fennel
2 tablespoons finely chopped parsley	2 tablespoons finely chopped parsley
1 small onion, finely sliced	1 small onion, finely sliced
1 box mustard and cress	1 box mustard and cress
4 tablespoons low-calorie French Dressing	4 tablespoons low-calorie French Dressing

Wash and finely slice the unpeeled cucumber and place in a salad bowl. Wash and grate the fennel and add to the cucumber with all the remaining ingredients. Toss lightly and serve.
Total Calories 76
18 Calories per portion

Stir-Fry Vegetables

METRIC/IMPERIAL	AMERICAN
1 tablespoon vegetable oil	1 tablespoon vegetable oil
1 onion, sliced	1 onion, sliced
3 celery sticks, sliced	3 stalks celery, sliced
½ green pepper, cored, seeded and cut into matchsticks	½ green pepper, cored, seeded and cut into matchsticks
2 carrots, cut into matchsticks	2 carrots, cut into matchsticks
½ cucumber, chopped	½ cucumber, chopped
225 g/8 oz bean sprouts	4 cups bean sprouts
1 tablespoon soy sauce	1 tablespoon soy sauce
10 drops liquid sweetener	10 drops liquid sweetener
2 tablespoons beef or chicken stock	2 tablespoons beef or chicken stock

Heat the oil in a large frying pan (skillet) or wok. Quickly fry the onion, celery, pepper and carrots for a few minutes, stirring continuously. Add the cucumber and bean sprouts and continue cooking for a further 2 to 3 minutes. Stir in the soy sauce, sweetener and stock. Heat for 2 minutes more, then serve immediately.
Serves 4
Total Calories 300
75 Calories per portion

'Cheat' Chips

METRIC/IMPERIAL	AMERICAN
750 g/1½ lb potatoes, boiled in their skins	1½ lb potatoes, boiled in their skins
salt	salt

When the potatoes are cool, remove the skins. Cut the potatoes into slices and spread them on the grill (broiler) pan. Sprinkle lightly with salt. Preheat the grill until it is very hot, then grill (broil) the potato slices until crisp and golden brown, turning once.
Serves 4
Total Calories 530
132 Calories per portion

Hot Artichokes with Piquant Sauce

METRIC/IMPERIAL	AMERICAN
2 globe artichokes, trimmed	2 globe artichokes, trimmed
Sauce:	**Sauce:**
½ green pepper, cored, seeded and diced	½ green pepper, cored, seeded and diced
1 celery stick, finely chopped	1 stalk celery, finely chopped
1 tablespoon finely chopped onion	1 tablespoon finely chopped onion
50 g/2 oz button mushrooms, chopped	½ cup button mushrooms, chopped
½ beef stock cube, crumbled	1 beef bouillon cube, crumbled
150 ml/¼ pint tomato juice	⅔ cup tomato juice
salt	salt
pinch of chilli powder	pinch of chili powder

Cook the artichokes in plenty of boiling salted water for 35 to 40 minutes. They are cooked when a leaf can be pulled out easily. Drain and keep hot.

To make the sauce, place all the ingredients in a saucepan and cook for 10 minutes, stirring occasionally. Pour into small serving bowls and serve with the artichokes so that the base of each leaf may be dipped in the sauce before eating.

Serves 2
Total Calories 85
42 Calories per portion

Special Stuffed Peppers

METRIC/IMPERIAL	AMERICAN
4 green peppers	4 green peppers
1 × 285 g/9½ oz can pear quarters in natural juice	1 × 9½ oz can pear quarters in natural juice
225 g/8 oz boiled rice	1½ cups boiled rice
1 × 285 g/9½ oz can prawns in brine, drained	1 × 9½ oz can shrimp in brine, drained
salt	salt
freshly ground black pepper	freshly ground black pepper
4 teaspoons vegetable oil	4 teaspoons vegetable oil

Cut the tops off the peppers and discard the cores and seeds. Cook the tops with the peppers in boiling water for about 5 minutes, making sure that they remain fairly firm. Drain the peppers and stand them in a baking tin (pan) or ovenproof dish.

Drain the pears, reserving the juice, and roughly chop. Mix the rice, prawns (shrimp) and pears together, add salt and pepper to taste and moisten with pear juice. Spoon the mixture into the pepper shells and replace the tops of the peppers. Brush with the oil, cover with foil and bake in a preheated moderate oven (180°C/350°F, Gas Mark 4) for 15 minutes.

Serves 4
Total Calories 855
214 Calories per portion

Courgette (Zucchini) and Tomato Salad

METRIC/IMPERIAL	AMERICAN
225 g/8 oz courgettes, sliced, lightly cooked and drained	½ lb zucchini, sliced, lightly cooked and drained
6 tomatoes, cut into wedges	6 tomatoes, cut into wedges
½ onion, finely chopped	½ onion, finely chopped
Dressing:	**Dressing:**
1 tablespoon wine vinegar	1 tablespoon wine vinegar
1 teaspoon sugar	1 teaspoon sugar
¼ teaspoon French mustard	¼ teaspoon Dijon-style mustard
1 × 150 g/5 oz carton plain yogurt	1 × 5 oz carton plain yogurt
½ tablespoon chopped fresh parsley or dill to garnish	½ tablespoon chopped fresh parsley or dill to garnish

Place the vegetables in a serving bowl and mix carefully together.

Make the dressing by blending all the ingredients in a bowl. Pour over the salad, then chill well in the refrigerator. Just before serving, garnish with chopped parsley or dill.

Serves 4
Total Calories 190
48 Calories per portion

SNACKS
AND DIPS

Baked Potatoes

Potatoes should not be ruled out when dieting. They are both nutritious and satisfying and with a filling, can make a balanced meal.

Choose even sized potatoes, if cooking more than one.

Scrub and dry the potatoes, then prick all over with a fork. Place on a baking sheet and bake in a preheated hot oven (200°C/400°F, Gas Mark 6) for 1 to 1¼ hours until tender when pierced with a knife.
Total Calories: 100 per 100 g/4 oz potato.

Serve with any one of the following delicious fillings.

Camembert Filling

METRIC/IMPERIAL For each potato:	AMERICAN For each potato:
50 g/2 oz Camembert cheese	⅛ lb Camembert cheese
50 g/2 oz cottage cheese	¼ cup cottage cheese
salt	salt
freshly ground black pepper	freshly ground black pepper

Remove the rind from the Camembert and mash with the cottage cheese and salt and pepper to taste.

Cut the potato in half, scoop out the flesh and combine with the cheese mixture.

Spoon back into the potato shells. Place under a preheated grill (broiler) for 2 minutes to heat through. Serve with salad.
230 Calories excluding potato

Baked Potatoes with Cottage Cheese, Camembert and Blue Cheese Fillings

Blue Cheese Filling

METRIC/IMPERIAL For each potato:	AMERICAN For each potato:
50 g/2 oz blue cheese, Danish or Stilton, crumbled	½ cup crumbled blue cheese, Danish or Stilton
4 teaspoons plain unsweetened yogurt	4 teaspoons plain unsweetened yogurt
salt	salt
freshly ground black pepper	freshly ground black pepper
lettuce to serve	lettuce to serve

Combine the cheese with the yogurt and salt and pepper to taste.

Cut a cross in the top of each potato and spoon on the cheese and yogurt mixture.

Return to the oven briefly to heat through. Serve on lettuce.
Danish Blue: 210 Calories excluding potato;
Stilton: 300 Calories excluding potato

Cottage Cheese Filling

METRIC/IMPERIAL For each potato:	AMERICAN For each potato:
50 g/2 oz cottage cheese	¼ cup cottage cheese
2 teaspoons tomato purée	2 teaspoons tomato paste
salt	salt
freshly ground black pepper	freshly ground black pepper

Mix the cottage cheese, tomato purée (paste) and salt and pepper to taste.

Cut the potato in half, scoop out the flesh and combine with the cheese mixture.

Spoon back into the potato shells and return to the oven for 2 minutes to heat through.
75 Calories excluding potato

Tuna Fish Fondue

METRIC/IMPERIAL	AMERICAN
½ clove garlic	½ clove garlic
1 teaspoon lemon juice	1 teaspoon lemon juice
300 ml/½ pint dry white wine	1¼ cups dry white wine
1 tablespoon cornflour	1 tablespoon cornstarch
400 g/14 oz Edam cheese, grated	3½ cups grated Edam cheese
1 × 200 g/7 oz can tuna in brine, drained and flaked	1 × 7 oz can tuna in brine, drained and flaked
freshly ground black pepper	freshly ground black pepper
pinch of grated nutmeg	pinch of grated nutmeg

Use the cut garlic clove to rub the inside of a heavy saucepan or fondue pan, then discard. Place the lemon juice in the pan and pour in the wine, reserving 2 tablespoons. Bring to the boil, then reduce the heat. Meanwhile, blend the cornflour (cornstarch) with the reserved wine to form a smooth paste.

Gradually add the grated cheese to the wine, stirring continuously, until the cheese has nearly melted. Stir in the cornflour (cornstarch) paste and continue cooking and stirring until smooth. Finally, stir in the tuna, pepper and nutmeg and serve immediately with a selection of bread and raw vegetables for dipping into the fondue.
Serves 6
Total Calories 1690
280 Calories per portion

Cottage Dip

METRIC/IMPERIAL	AMERICAN
225 g/8 oz cottage cheese	1 cup cottage cheese
1 red pepper, cored, seeded and finely chopped	1 red pepper, cored, seeded and finely chopped
1 green dessert apple, cored and finely chopped	1 green dessert apple, cored and finely chopped
50 g/2 oz mixed nuts and raisins	⅓ cup mixed nuts and raisins
few drops Tabasco sauce	few drops hot pepper sauce
1 teaspoon lemon juice	1 teaspoon lemon juice
salt	salt
freshly ground black pepper	freshly ground black pepper
biscuits or crispbreads to serve	crackers or crispbreads to serve
thin slices of red pepper to garnish	thin slices of red pepper to garnish

Mix all the ingredients for the dip together. Spoon into a bowl and place in the centre of a large platter with the biscuits or crispbreads arranged around the bowl. Garnish with thin slices of red pepper.
Total Calories 585 (without biscuits or crispbreads)

Avocado Dip

METRIC/IMPERIAL	AMERICAN
1 ripe avocado	1 ripe avocado
1 teaspoon lemon juice	1 teaspoon lemon juice
few drops angostura bitters (optional)	few drops angostura bitters (optional)
100 g/4 oz low-fat soft cheese	½ cup low-fat soft cheese
salt	salt
freshly ground black pepper	freshly ground black pepper
To garnish:	**To garnish:**
twist of lemon	twist of lemon
pinch of paprika	pinch of paprika

Peel and stone (seed) the avocado and mash until creamy and smooth. Add the lemon juice, bitters (if using), cheese and salt and pepper to taste. Mix well and spoon into a serving dish. Garnish with a twist of lemon and a dusting of paprika.
Total Calories 325

Calorie-Counters' Fondue

METRIC/IMPERIAL	AMERICAN
1 clove garlic, crushed	1 clove garlic, crushed
200 ml/⅓ pint skimmed	⅞ cup skim milk
450 g/1 lb Edam or low-fat cheese, grated	4 cups grated Edam or low-fat cheese
4 teaspoons cornflour	4 teaspoons cornstarch
salt	salt
freshly ground black pepper	freshly ground black pepper

Place the garlic and milk in a large saucepan and heat gently. Toss together the cheese and the cornflour (cornstarch) and gradually add to the milk. Stir continuously as the cheese melts. Add salt and pepper to taste. Keep the fondue warm, but not boiling, for serving. Serve with celery sticks, carrot wedges and cauliflower florets for dipping into the fondue.
Serves 4
Total Calories 1550
388 Calories per portion

Aubergine (Eggplant) Dip

METRIC/IMPERIAL	AMERICAN
1 aubergine	1 eggplant
225 g/8 oz low-fat soft cheese	1 cup low-fat soft cheese
6-7 spring onions, finely chopped	6-7 scallions, finely chopped
2 teaspoons finely chopped fresh parsley	2 teaspoons finely chopped fresh parsley
salt	salt
freshly ground black pepper	freshly ground black pepper
To garnish:	**To garnish:**
few stuffed olives	few stuffed olives
1 gherkin, sliced	1 gherkin, sliced

Prick the aubergine (eggplant) with a fork and bake in a preheated moderately hot oven (190°C/375°F, Gas Mark 5) for 40 to 50 minutes, until tender. Leave to cool.

Halve the aubergine (eggplant) and scoop the flesh out into a bowl. Mash well and mix in the cheese, onions and parsley and salt and pepper to taste. Spoon into a serving dish and garnish with olives and gherkin slices. Serve with fresh crusty bread or biscuits and raw vegetables, eg. carrot sticks, cauliflower florets and cucumber wedges, for dipping.
Total Calories 270 (without bread, biscuits or vegetable dippers)

Potted Cheese

METRIC/IMPERIAL	AMERICAN
175 g/6 oz cottage cheese	¾ cup cottage cheese
50 g/2 oz low-fat soft cheese	¼ cup low-fat soft cheese
½ teaspoon French mustard	½ teaspoon Dijon-style mustard
pinch of garlic salt	pinch of garlic salt

Mash the cottage cheese with the low-fat soft cheese until smooth. Mix in the mustard and garlic salt. Spoon into a serving dish and serve with a ploughman's platter.

Vary the flavour of the cheese by adding 1 teaspoon Worcestershire sauce or ½ teaspoon tomato purée (paste) instead of the mustard.
Serves 2
Total Calories 215
107 Calories per portion

Crab Dip

METRIC/IMPERIAL	AMERICAN
1 × 185 g/6½ oz can crabmeat	1 × 6½ oz can crabmeat
100 g/4 oz celery, finely chopped	1 cup finely chopped celery
2 hard-boiled eggs, finely chopped	2 hard-cooked eggs, finely chopped
2 tablespoons finely chopped onion	2 tablespoons finely chopped onion
200 ml/⅓ pint low-calorie mayonnaise	scant 1 cup low-calorie mayonnaise
pinch of grated nutmeg	pinch of grated nutmeg
1 tablespoon lemon juice	1 tablespoon lemon juice
salt	salt
freshly ground black pepper	freshly ground black pepper
To serve:	**To serve:**
celery sticks	celery stalks
cucumber	cucumber
green pepper	green pepper
cocktail biscuits	cocktail crackers

Drain the crabmeat and flake into a bowl. Stir in the celery, egg, onion and mayonnaise. Add nutmeg, lemon juice and salt and pepper to taste.

Spoon into a serving bowl in the centre of a large platter. Cut the celery, cucumber and green pepper into strips and arrange round the bowl with the biscuits for dipping.
Total Calories 875 (without vegetable dippers)

Summer Filled Pitta Bread

METRIC/IMPERIAL	AMERICAN
1 wholewheat or white pitta bread	1 wholewheat or white pitta bread
1 teaspoon low-fat spread	1 teaspoon low-fat spread
25 g/1 oz French beans, cooked and chopped	¼ cup green beans, cooked and chopped
50 g/2 oz tuna fish in brine, flaked	¼ cup tuna fish in brine, flaked
25 g/1 oz red pepper, chopped	1 tablespoon chopped red pepper
25 g/1 oz green pepper, chopped	1 tablespoon chopped green pepper
4 black olives, stoned	4 pitted ripe olives
salt	salt
freshly ground black pepper	freshly ground black pepper

Slit the pitta bread down one side and spread the inside with the low-fat spread. Mix the remaining ingredients together with salt and pepper to taste and spoon into the bread. Serve immediately.
Serves 1
Total Calories 270

Prawn (Shrimp) Sandwiches

METRIC/IMPERIAL	AMERICAN
100 g/4 oz prawns, peeled and chopped	¾ cup chopped shelled shrimp
2 tablespoons low-calorie mayonnaise	2 tablespoons low-calorie mayonnaise
1 teaspoon snipped chives	1 teaspoon snipped chives
4 slices wholewheat bread	4 slices wholewheat bread

Combine the prawns (shrimp) and mayonnaise in a bowl. Stir in the chives.

Divide the prawn (shrimp) mixture between two slices of bread. Top with the remaining slices. Cut each into quarters.
Serves 2
Total Calories 520
130 Calories per portion

Crunchy Open Sandwiches

METRIC/IMPERIAL	AMERICAN
2 slices rye, black or pumpernickel bread	2 slices rye, black or pumpernickel bread
15 g/½ oz low-fat spread	1 tablespoon low-fat spread
Topping 1:	**Topping 1:**
2 slices lean roast beef	2 slices lean roast beef
2 asparagus spears, cooked	2 asparagus spears, cooked
2 slices stuffed olive	2 slices stuffed olive
Topping 2:	**Topping 2:**
2 slices ham	2 slices ham
¼ red dessert apple, sliced	¼ red dessert apple, sliced
¼ green dessert apple, sliced	¼ green dessert apple sliced
Topping 3:	**Topping 3:**
100 g/4 oz cottage cheese	½ cup cottage cheese
2 apricot halves (or other fruit)	2 apricot halves (or other fruit)
Topping 4:	**Topping 4:**
4 slices cold cooked chicken	4 slices cold cooked chicken
½ small avocado, peeled and sliced	½ small avocado, peeled and sliced

Spread the bread lightly with the low-fat spread. Choose one of the toppings and arrange the ingredients attractively on top of the bread slices.
Serves 2

Topping 1
Total Calories 270
135 Calories per portion
Topping 2
Total Calories 285
143 Calories per portion

Topping 3
Total Calories 290
145 Calories per portion
Topping 4
Total Calories 425
212 Calories per portion

Prawn (Shrimp) Sandwiches
Summer Filled Pitta Bread
Crunchy Open Sandwiches
(Photograph: St Ivel Gold)

Egg Ramekins

METRIC/IMPERIAL	AMERICAN
4 tomatoes, peeled and chopped	4 tomatoes, peeled and chopped
2 tablespoons chopped fresh chives	2 tablespoons chopped fresh chives
salt	salt
freshly ground black pepper	freshly ground black pepper
4 eggs	4 eggs
4 tablespoons low-fat spread	4 tablespoons low-fat spread
1 tablepoon chopped fresh parsley to garnish	1 tablespoon chopped fresh parsley to garnish

Divide the tomatoes between four ramekin dishes. Add the chives and salt and pepper to taste. Break an egg into each dish and top with 1 tablespoon low-fat spread. Bake in a preheated hot oven (220°C/425°F, Gas Mark 7) for 15 minutes, until the eggs have set. Serve immediately, garnished with chopped parsley.
Serves 4
Total Calories 535
134 Calories per portion

Devilled Desk-top Wheels

METRIC/IMPERIAL	AMERICAN
100 g/4 oz ham, finely chopped	½ cup finely chopped ham
1 teaspoon low-fat spread	1 teaspoon low-fat spread
1 teaspoon coarse-grained mustard	1 teaspoon coarse-grained mustard
dash of Worcestershire sauce	dash of Worcestershire sauce
freshly ground black pepper	freshly ground black pepper
4 slices white bread	4 slices white bread
4 slices wholewheat bread	4 slices wholewheat bread

Combine the ham, spread, mustard, Worcestershire sauce and pepper and spread evenly over the slices of white bread. Top with the wholewheat bread. Using a 10 cm/4 inch cutter, cut each sandwich into a round. Cut a 5 cm/2 inch round from the centre of each sandwich, reverse and replace to give a contrasting centre.
Serves 2 to 4
Total Calories 680
340 to 170 Calories per portion

Cocktail Kebabs (Kabobs)

METRIC/IMPERIAL	AMERICAN
50 g/2 oz smoked salmon	¼ cup smoked salmon
3 slices wholewheat bread	3 slices wholewheat bread
15 g/½ oz low-fat spread	1 tablespoon low-fat spread
½ melon, seeded and cubed	½ melon, seeded and cubed
lemon wedges to garnish	lemon wedges to garnish

Trim the smoked salmon into 2 × 5 cm/¾ × 2 inch strips and roll up. Spread the bread with the low-fat spread and cut into squares. Thread the salmon rolls, bread and melon alternately on to cocktail sticks (toothpicks). Garnish with lemon wedges to serve.
Makes about 12 kebabs (kabobs)
Total Calories 415
35 Calories per portion

Chicken Toasties

METRIC/IMPERIAL	AMERICAN
100 g/4 oz cold cooked chicken, diced	½ cup diced cold cooked chicken
100 g/4 oz cooked sweetcorn	¾ cup cooked whole kernel corn
6 tablespoons low-calorie mayonnaise	6 tablespoons low-calorie mayonnaise
8 slices wholewheat bread	8 slices wholewheat bread
25 g/1 oz low-fat spread	2 tablespoons low-fat spread

Combine the chicken, sweetcorn and mayonnaise. Spread the bread with the low-fat spread and trim to fit a sandwich toaster. Place the bread 'sunnyside down' in the toaster and spoon some of the filling into the centre. Place another slice of bread 'sunnyside up' on top and cook according to the toaster manufacturer's instructions.
Serves 2 to 4
Total Calories 1245
622 to 311 Calories per portion

Low-Calorie Lunch

METRIC/IMPERIAL	AMERICAN
100 g/4 oz cottage cheese	½ cup cottage cheese
50 g/2 oz cucumber, chopped	½ cup chopped cucumber
50 g/2 oz celery, chopped	½ cup chopped celery
50 g/2 oz carrot, chopped	½ cup chopped carrot
½ dessert apple, cored and chopped	½ dessert apple, cored and chopped
few capers	few capers
1 gherkin, chopped	1 gherkin, chopped
few drops Tabasco sauce	few drops hot pepper sauce

Mix all the ingredients together, adding Tabasco (hot pepper) sauce to taste. Serve with crusty wholewheat bread or a selection of crispbreads.
Serves 1
Total Calories 160

Cheese with Prawns (Shrimp) and Asparagus

METRIC/IMPERIAL	AMERICAN
450 g/1 lb cottage cheese	2 cups cottage cheese
225 g/8 oz prawns, peeled	1⅓ cups shelled shrimp
salt	salt
freshly ground black pepper	freshly ground black pepper
1 cucumber, peeled and diced	1 cucumber, peeled and diced
1 × 225 g/8 oz can asparagus spears, drained and chopped	1 × 8 oz can asparagus spears, drained and chopped
lettuce leaves to serve	lettuce leaves to serve

Place the cottage cheese and prawns (shrimp) in a bowl and mix together. Add salt and pepper to taste. Stir in the cucumber and asparagus.

Divide the lettuce leaves between four plates. Divide the cottage cheese mixture into four and spoon onto the lettuce beds. Serve immediately.
Serves 4
Total Calories 520
130 Calories per portion

Easy Pasta

METRIC/IMPERIAL	AMERICAN
225 g/8 oz pasta shapes	2 cups pasta shapes
225 g/8 oz cottage cheese	1 cup cottage cheese
100 g/4 oz cooked ham, chopped	½ cup chopped cooked ham
1 tablespoon finely chopped mixed fresh herbs	1 tablespoon finely chopped mixed fresh herbs
pinch of garlic salt	pinch of garlic salt
freshly ground black pepper	freshly ground black pepper

Cook the pasta shapes in boiling salted water until tender, then drain well. Mix the cheese, ham, herbs, garlic salt and pepper together, add to the freshly cooked pasta and toss lightly. Serve immediately.

This recipe may be varied, if liked, by adding prawns (shrimp), diced cooked chicken, or canned fish in brine, instead of the ham.
Serves 4
Total Calories 1245
311 Calories per portion

Cheese and Tomato Toast

METRIC/IMPERIAL	AMERICAN
4 slices bread	4 slices bread
175 g/6 oz cheese, grated	1½ cups grated cheese
4 teaspoons tomato purée	4 teaspoons tomato paste
4 small tomatoes, sliced	4 small tomatoes, sliced

Toast the bread under a preheated hot grill (broiler) on one side only.

Mix the cheese and tomato purée (paste) together and spread onto the untoasted side of the bread.

Return to the grill (broiler) and when the mixture is bubbling, place the sliced tomatoes on top.

Grill (broil) until the tomatoes are soft.
Serves 4
Total Calories 250
62 Calories per portion

LOW CALORIE DESSERTS

Omelette Soufflé with Strawberries

METRIC/IMPERIAL	AMERICAN
2 eggs, separated	2 eggs, separated
6 drops liquid sweetener	6 drops liquid sweetener
2 tablespoons water	2 tablespoons water
1 teaspoon melted butter	1 teaspoon melted butter
100 g/4 oz strawberries, hulled and halved	¼ lb strawberries, hulled and halved
To decorate:	**To decorate:**
mint sprigs	mint sprigs
strawberry	strawberry

Whisk the egg yolks until creamy, then fold in the water and liquid sweetener.

Whisk the egg whites until very stiff and gently fold into the egg yolk mixture with a metal spoon.

Heat the melted butter in a frying pan (skillet) making sure the base and sides are well greased. Pour in the egg mixture.

Cook over a low heat until the underside is golden brown. Place the strawberries in the centre of the omelette and fold the omelette in half.

Serve immediately on a warmed plate. Decorate with a mint sprig and a strawberry.

Serves 1
Total Calories 180

Blackcurrant Fool

METRIC/IMPERIAL	AMERICAN
450 g/1 lb blackcurrants	1 lb black currants
150 ml/¼ pint unsweetened apple juice	⅔ cup unsweetened apple juice
2 tablespoons custard powder	2 tablespoons Birds English dessert mix
300 ml/½ pint skimmed milk	1¼ cups skim milk
40 drops liquid sweetener	40 drops liquid sweetener
1 × 150 g/5.3 oz carton unsweetened blackcurrant yogurt	⅔ cup black currant yogurt
To decorate:	**To decorate:**
few blackcurrants	few black currants
few mint sprigs	few mint sprigs

Place the blackcurrants in a saucepan with the apple juice. Cook over a low heat for about 10 minutes. Remove from the heat and leave to cool.

Blend the custard powder (dessert mix) with a little of the skimmed milk. Heat the remaining milk and stir into the custard mixture, then return to the pan. Bring to the boil, stirring constantly, and cook for 1 minute. Pour into a basin, cover the surface with wet greaseproof (waxed) paper to prevent a skin forming. Leave to cool.

Purée the blackcurrants in a blender or food processor and sieve to remove the skins. Add the custard and liquid sweetener to taste to the blackcurrant purée and whisk until well blended. Swirl in the yogurt and divide between four glasses and chill. Decorate with the mint sprigs and blackcurrants.

Serves 4
Total Calories 500
125 Calories per portion

Blackcurrant Fool
Omelette Soufflé with Strawberries
(Photograph: Sweetex)

Rosy Pears

METRIC/IMPERIAL
4 large firm pears, peeled, cored and quartered
250 ml/8 fl oz orange juice
120 ml/4 fl oz red wine
20 to 30 cardamom seeds
liquid sweetener, to taste (optional)

AMERICAN
4 large firm pears, peeled, cored and quartered
1 cup orange juice
½ cup red wine
20 to 30 cardamom seeds
liquid sweetener, to taste (optional)

Place the pears in a soufflé dish and pour on the orange juice and red wine.

Crack each cardamom seed with the back of a spoon and add to the dish.

Bake in a preheated moderately hot oven (200°C/400°F, Gas Mark 6) for about 30 minutes, depending on the hardness of the pears.

When cooked, taste for sweetness and, if liked, add liquid sweetener.

Serve hot or chilled, with plain unsweetened yogurt.
Serves 4
Total Calories 400
100 Calories per portion

Orange Pots

METRIC/IMPERIAL
2 tablespoons orange juice
4 teaspoons lemon juice
4 teaspoons powdered gelatine
350 g/12 oz cottage cheese
6 tablespoons buttermilk
liquid sweetener
1 orange, thinly sliced to decorate

AMERICAN
2 tablespoons orange juice
4 teaspoons lemon juice
4 teaspoons powdered gelatin
1½ cups cottage cheese
6 tablespoons buttermilk
liquid sweetener
1 orange, thinly sliced to decorate

Put the orange and lemon juices in a small bowl. Sprinkle the gelatine over the top and stand over a bowl of hot, but not boiling water, and stir until the gelatine dissolves.

Put the gelatine mixture into a blender with the cottage cheese and buttermilk and blend until smooth. Add liquid sweetener to taste.

Divide between four dessert glasses and decorate with orange slices.
Serves 4
Total Calories 540
135 Calories per portion

Raspberry Yogurt Whirl

METRIC/IMPERIAL
600 ml/1 pint plain yogurt
450 g/1 lb frozen raspberries, thawed
3-4 teaspoons artificial sweetener granules

AMERICAN
2½ cups plain yogurt
3 cups frozen raspberries thawed
3-4 teaspoons artificial sweetener granules

Place the yogurt and raspberries in a blender or food processor, reserving a few raspberries for decoration. Add sweetener to taste and process until smooth. Spoon into four individual dishes and decorate with the reserved raspberries.
Serves 4
Total Calories 420
105 Calories per portion

Blackcurrant and Mint Crumble

METRIC/IMPERIAL
1 × 300 g/10 oz can blackcurrants in natural juice
2 tablespoons chopped fresh mint
100 g/4 oz white breadcrumbs
1 tablespoon caster sugar
150 g/5 oz cottage cheese
6 teaspoons desiccated coconut

AMERICAN
1 × 10 oz can black currants in natural juice
2 tablespoons chopped fresh mint
2 cups white bread crumbs
1 tablespoon superfine sugar
⅔ cup cottage cheese
6 teaspoons shredded coconut

Place the blackcurrants in a saucepan with the mint and bring to the boil. Pour into an ovenproof dish. Mix the breadcrumbs, sugar, cottage cheese and coconut together and spoon over the blackcurrants. Bake in a preheated moderately hot oven (200°C/400°F, Gas Mark 6) for 20 minutes until golden brown.
Serves 4
Total Calories 750
188 Calories per portion

Exotic Fruit Salad

METRIC/IMPERIAL	AMERICAN
1 large pineapple	1 large pineapple
75 g/3 oz dates, stoned and halved	½ cup pitted dates, halved
75 g/3 oz strawberries, hulled and halved	½ cup strawberries, hulled and halved
2 kiwifruit, peeled and sliced	2 kiwifruit, peeled and sliced
50 g/2 oz grapes, halved and seeded	½ cup grapes, halved and pitted
1 tablespoon Kirsch (optional)	1 tablespoon Kirsch (optional)

Cut the pineapple in half lengthwise and scoop out the flesh, discarding the core, leaving a thin shell. Cut the flesh into neat pieces. Fill the shell with the fruits, then sprinkle over the Kirsch, if used. Chill for 1 to 2 hours before serving.
Serves 4
Total Calories 380 (without Kirsch – 410 Calories with Kirsch)
95 Calories per portion

Apricot Soufflé

METRIC/IMPERIAL	AMERICAN
1 × 227 g/8 oz can apricots in natural juice, drained	1 × 8 oz can apricots in natural juice, drained
2 eggs, separated	2 eggs, separated
2 teaspoons artificial sweetener granules	2 teaspoons artificial sweetener granules
15 g/½ oz powdered gelatine	2 envelopes unflavored gelatin
1 tablespoon lemon juice	1 tablespoon lemon juice
1 × 170 g/6 oz can evaporated milk	1 × 6 oz can evaporated milk

Reserve one or two apricots for decoration and purée the remainder in a blender or food processor or by pressing through a sieve.

Place the apricot purée in a heavy saucepan with the egg yolks and cook over a low heat, stirring lightly, until thickened. Remove from the heat and stir in the sweetener. Sprinkle the gelatine over and stir to dissolve. Add lemon juice to taste and cool until beginning to thicken.

Whip the evaporated milk until it holds its shape, then fold in the apricot mixture. Turn into four individual glasses and chill. Decorate with delicate slices of the reserved apricots.
Serves 4
Total Calories 600
150 Calories per portion

Grapefruit Sorbet

METRIC/IMPERIAL	AMERICAN
1 × 540 g/16½ oz can grapefruit segments in natural juice	1 × 16½ oz can grapefruit segments in natural juice
25 g/1 oz honey	1½ tablespoons honey
300 ml/½ pint water	1¼ cups water
finely grated rind of 2 lemons	finely grated rind of 2 lemons
150 ml/¼ pint lemon juice	⅔ cup lemon juice
2 egg whites	2 egg whites

Pass the grapefruit segments through a sieve and retain the juice.

Place the honey and water in a saucepan, bring to the boil and boil for 5 minutes. Cool slightly, then add the grapefruit juices, lemon rind and lemon juice. Cool and transfer to a shallow freezing container or ice tray. Freeze until half frozen. Whisk the egg whites until stiff. Turn the half frozen sorbet into a bowl and fold in the egg whites. Freeze again until firm.
Serves 6 to 8
Total Calories 325
54 to 41 Calories per portion

Lemon Cheesecake

METRIC/IMPERIAL	AMERICAN
75 g/3 oz digestive biscuit crumbs	¾ cup graham cracker crumbs
25 g/1 oz low-fat spread, melted	2 tablespoons low-fat spread, melted
15 g/½ oz powdered gelatine	2 envelopes unflavored gelatin
4 tablespoons hot water	4 tablespoons hot water
225 g/8 oz low-fat curd cheese	1 cup low-fat small curd cottage cheese
2 × 150 g/5 oz cartons plain yogurt	2 × 5 oz cartons plain yogurt
2 tablespoons lemon juice	2 tablespoons lemon juice
35 drops liquid sweetener	35 drops liquid sweetener
1 tablespoon lemon curd to decorate	1 tablespoon lemon curd to decorate

Mix the biscuit crumbs with the melted low-fat spread and press into the bottom of a 15 cm/6 inch round loose-bottomed cake tin (springform pan).

Sprinkle the gelatine over the hot water and stir to dissolve. Mix the cheese, yogurt, lemon juice and sweetener together, then add the gelatine. Check the flavouring, adding more sweetener if necessary, pour into the cake tin and leave to set in the refrigerator. To decorate, warm the lemon curd slightly and pour on top of the cheesecake in a swirl pattern.
Serves 8
Total Calories 1190
149 Calories per portion

Strawberry Water Ice

METRIC/IMPERIAL	AMERICAN
450 g/1 lb strawberries, hulled	1 lb strawberries, hulled
300 ml/½ pint low-calorie lemonade	1¼ cups low-calorie lemonade
36 drops liquid sweetener	36 drops liquid sweetener
1 egg white, beaten	1 egg white, beaten

Purée the strawberries in a blender or food processor, or press them through a sieve. Mix the strawberries with the lemonade and sweetener and transfer to a shallow freezer container or ice tray.

Freeze until almost set, then turn into a bowl and stir in the egg white. Return to the freezer until firm.
Serves 4 to 6
Total Calories 150
37 to 25 Calories per portion

Gooseberry Fool

METRIC/IMPERIAL	AMERICAN
450 g/1 lb gooseberries, cooked and puréed	1 lb gooseberries, cooked and puréed
70 drops liquid sweetener	70 drops liquid sweetener
150 ml/¼ pint plain yogurt	⅔ cup plain yogurt
150 ml/¼ pint skimmed milk	⅔ cup skim milk
1 egg, lightly beaten	1 egg, lightly beaten

Mix the gooseberry purée with the sweetener to taste, then fold in the yogurt. Heat the milk with the egg in the top of a double saucepan (double boiler), stirring constantly until the custard thickens. Fold in the gooseberry mixture, transfer to a serving dish and leave to set.
Serves 4
Total Calories 300
75 Calories per portion

Loganberry Meringue Flan (Pie)

METRIC/IMPERIAL	AMERICAN
Base:	**Base:**
4 egg whites	4 egg whites
250 g/8 oz icing sugar, sieved	scant 2 cups sifted confectioners' sugar
few drops vanilla essence	few drops vanilla
Filling:	**Filling:**
750 g/1½ lb loganberries	5 cups loganberries

Place the egg whites and icing (confectioners') sugar in a heatproof bowl over a pan of hot water. Whisk until the mixture is very thick and holds its shape (this will take at least 10 minutes). Add the vanilla to taste.

Spoon the meringue into a piping (pastry) bag fitted with a 1 cm/½ inch star nozzle and pipe a 20 cm/ 8 inch round on a baking sheet lined with non-stick (parchment) paper. Then pipe around the edge to build up the sides.

Cook in a cool oven (140°C/275°F, Gas Mark 1) for 50 minutes until set and crisp. Remove from the oven, leave to cool and remove paper. Fill with loganberries just before serving.
Serves 8
Total Calories 1120
140 Calories per portion

Loganberry Meringue Flan (Pie)

Surprise Oranges

METRIC/IMPERIAL	AMERICAN
4 oranges	4 oranges
1 banana	1 banana
1 dessert apple	1 dessert apple
1 teaspoon artificial sweetener granules	1 teaspoon artificial sweetener granules

Cut a thin slice from the base of each orange so that they will stand firmly. Cut off the tops so that the flesh is just showing and scoop out all the flesh with a teaspoon, discarding any pips. Finely chop the banana and apple and add to the orange flesh, with sweetener to taste. Pile back into the orange shells and chill in the refrigerator before serving.
Serves 4
Total Calories 370
93 Calories per portion

Slimmers' Apple and Orange Dessert

METRIC/IMPERIAL	AMERICAN
450 g/1 lb cooking apples, peeled, cored and chopped	1 lb tart apples, peeled, cored and chopped
juice of 1 large orange	juice of 1 large orange
few drops liquid sweetener	few drops liquid sweetener
150 ml/¼ pint plain yogurt	⅔ cup plain yogurt
3 tablespoons Special K cereal	3 tablespoons Special K cereal

Place the apples in a saucepan and pour over the orange juice. Add sweetener to taste, then simmer gently until the apple is soft, but retains its shape. Leave to cool, then divide among four small dessert glasses. Top each with yogurt and sprinkle with cereal.
Serves 4
Total Calories 300
75 Calories per portion

Jamaican Bananas

METRIC/IMPERIAL	AMERICAN
4 small bananas	4 small bananas
2 teaspoons lemon juice	2 teaspoons lemon juice
25 g/1 oz low-fat spread	2 tablespoons low-fat spread
grated rind and juice of 1 orange	grated rind and juice of 1 orange
pinch of ground cinnamon	pinch of ground cinnamon
2 teaspoons rum or few drops rum essence	2 teaspoons rum or few drops rum extract
few drops liquid sweetener	few drops liquid sweetener
25 g/1 oz flaked almonds, toasted	¼ cup slivered almonds, toasted

Peel the bananas and brush with lemon juice. Melt the low-fat spread in a large frying pan (skillet) and sauté the bananas on both sides until golden brown. Place the bananas on a serving dish and keep hot.

Place the orange rind and juice, cinnamon, rum and sweetener in the pan and bring to the boil. Cook for a few minutes then pour over the bananas. Sprinkle with toasted almonds and serve immediately.
Serves 4
Total Calories 515
129 Calories per portion

Blackberry Baked Apples

METRIC/IMPERIAL	AMERICAN
4 large cooking apples, cored	4 large tart apples, cored
4 slices low-calorie bread, crumbed	4 slices low-calorie bread, crumbed
grated rind and juice of 1 orange	grated rind and juice of 1 orange
pinch of ground cinnamon	pinch of ground cinnamon
100 g/4 oz blackberries	2/3 cup blackberries
few drops liquid sweetener	few drops liquid sweetener

Score the apple skins horizontally around the middle and stand each on a piece of foil. Mix together the remaining ingredients, adding sweetener to taste, and pile into the cavities of the apples. Wrap each apple in foil and place in an ovenproof dish.

Bake in a preheated moderately hot oven (190°C/375°F, Gas Mark 5) for 30 to 40 minutes, until tender.
Serves 4
Total Calories 550
137 Calories per portion

Queen of Puddings

METRIC/IMPERIAL	AMERICAN
150 ml/1/4 pint skimmed milk	2/3 cup skim milk
2 egg yolks	2 egg yolks
100 g/4 oz breadcrumbs	2 cups bread crumbs
3 drops liquid sweetener	3 drops liquid sweetener
450 g/1 lb stewed apples or pears	1 lb stewed apples or pears
Topping:	**Topping:**
2 egg whites	2 egg whites
2 drops liquid sweetener	2 drops liquid sweetener

Heat the milk until lukewarm, then add the egg yolks, breadcrumbs and sweetener. Mix well and pour into an ovenproof dish. Bake in a preheated moderate oven (180°C/350°F, Gas Mark 4) for about 30 minutes, until lightly set. Cover with the apples or pears.

To make the topping, whisk the egg whites until stiff, then fold in the sweetener. Pile on top of the pudding and return to the oven until set. Serve immediately.
Serve 4
Total Calories 650
163 Calories per portion

Easy Chocolate Pudding

METRIC/IMPERIAL	AMERICAN
50 g/2 oz ground rice	1/3 cup ground rice
25 g/1 oz cocoa powder	1/4 cup unsweetened cocoa
few drops liquid sweetener to taste	few drops liquid sweetener to taste
600 ml/1 pint skimmed milk	2 1/2 cups skim milk

Mix the ground rice and cocoa to a smooth paste with the sweetener and a quarter of the milk. Heat the remaining milk to boiling point, then pour over the rice mixture. Stir well, then return to the pan. Continue stirring whilst the mixture thickens and simmer for 3 to 4 minutes. Serve hot.
Serves 4
Total Calories 490
122 Calories per portion

Pavlova

METRIC/IMPERIAL	AMERICAN
3 egg whites	3 egg whites
1 teaspoon cream of tartar	1 teaspoon cream of tartar
3 tablespoons skimmed milk powder	3 tablespoons skim milk powder
liquid sweetener, to taste	liquid sweetener, to taste
450 g/1 lb mixed soft fruit (eg strawberries, kiwifruit, grapes, etc)	1 lb mixed soft fruit (eg strawberries, kiwifruit, grapes, etc)

Beat the egg whites and cream of tartar until stiff. Fold in the skimmed milk powder and liquid sweetener.

Cover a baking sheet with foil and lightly brush with oil. Pile the mixture onto the baking sheet and then flatten into a circle.

Bake in a preheated very cool oven (150°C/300°F, Gas Mark 2) for about 30 minutes. Cool and loosen carefully.

Arrange the fruit on top of the meringue and serve immediately.
95 Calories for the meringue

DIET DRINKS

'C' Frisco

METRIC/IMPERIAL	AMERICAN
2 tablespoons unsweetened orange juice	2 tablespoons unsweetened orange juice
1 tablespoon lemon juice	1 tablespoon lemon juice
2 tablespoons unsweetened grapefruit juice	2 tablespoons unsweetened grapefruit juice
2 tablespoons unsweetened pineapple juice	2 tablespoons unsweetened pineapple juice
1 egg white	1 egg white
ice	ice
To decorate:	**To decorate:**
pineapple slice	pineapple slice
cocktail cherry	cocktail cherry

Place all the ingredients in a cocktail shaker or blender. Shake or blend to combine.

Pour into a glass and decorate with a pineapple slice and a cocktail cherry.

Serves 1
Total Calories 46

Cool Cup

METRIC/IMPERIAL	AMERICAN
4 tablespoons blackcurrant cordial	4 tablespoons black currant cordial
350 ml/12 fl oz dry white wine, chilled	1½ cups dry white wine, chilled
600 ml/1 pint sparkling mineral water	2½ cups sparkling mineral water
crushed ice	crushed ice
mint sprigs	mint sprigs

Pour the blackcurrant cordial into a large jug. Add the chilled wine, mineral water, crushed ice and mint sprigs.

Serve immediately in chilled glasses.

Serves 8
Total Calories 455
57 Calories per portion

Dew Delight

METRIC/IMPERIAL	AMERICAN
250 ml/8 fl oz lemon juice	1 cup lemon juice
450 ml/¾ pint unsweetened grapefruit juice	2 cups unsweetened grapefruit juice
900 ml/1½ pints unsweetened apple juice	3¾ cups unsweetened apple juice
grenadine (optional)	grenadine (optional)
To decorate:	**To decorate:**
apple slices	apple slices
mint sprigs	mint sprigs

Combine the lemon, grapefruit and apple juices in a mug. Mix well. Add two dashes of grenadine (if using).

Serve in tall glasses, decorated with apple slices and mint sprigs.

Serves 4
Total Calories 140
35 Calories per portion

'C' Frisco, Cool Cup, Dew Delight
(Photograph: Ashbourne Natural Water and Libby's 'C' Drinks)

Fresh Lemonade

METRIC/IMPERIAL	AMERICAN
grated rind and juice of 4 lemons	grated rind and juice of 4 lemons
few drops liquid sweetener or 1 sweetener tablet, crushed	few drops liquid sweetener or 1 sweetener tablet, crushed
900 ml/1½ pints boiling water	3¾ cups boiling water
To serve:	**To serve:**
ice cubes	ice cubes
lemon slices	lemon slices
1 sprig mint	1 sprig mint

Place the lemon rind in a large jug with the sweetener. Pour over the boiling water and leave to cool. Add the lemon juice and refrigerate until required.

To serve, strain the lemonade into a tall glass jug, add ice cubes and decorate with lemon slices and mint.
Serves 4 to 6
Total Calories 10
Negligible Calories per portion

Honey Wheat Grapefruit Sip

METRIC/IMPERIAL	AMERICAN
1 × 540 g/17½ oz can grapefruit segments in natural juice	1 × 17½ oz can grapefruit segments in natural juice
3 tablespoons wheatgerm	3 tablespoons wheatgerm
4-5 teaspoons honey	4-5 teaspoons honey
150 ml/¼ pint skimmed milk	⅔ cup skim milk
2 scoops low-calorie ice cream	2 scoops low-calorie ice cream

Put the grapefruit and juice, wheatgerm and honey into a blender or food processor and blend until smooth. Leave for 10 minutes for the wheatgerm to soften, then add the milk and blend again until frothy. Pour into glasses and serve topped with ice cream.

For even fewer calories, use a sweetening substitute instead of the honey.
Serves 2
Total Calories 455
227 Calories per portion

Planters' Punch

METRIC/IMPERIAL	AMERICAN
600 ml/1 pint iced tea	2½ cups iced tea
600 ml/1 pint orange juice	2½ cups orange juice
150 ml/¼ pint lemon juice	⅔ cup lemon juice
dash of brandy (optional)	dash of brandy (optional)
slices of apple, orange and lemon to decorate	slices of apple, orange and lemon to decorate

Mix all the ingredients, except the fruit slices. Serve in tall glasses with straws, decorated with fruit slices.
Serves 4-6
Total Calories 220
55 to 36 Calories per portion

Pink Tonic

METRIC/IMPERIAL	AMERICAN
1 litre/1¾ pints low-calorie tonic water	4¼ cups low-calorie tonic water
few drops of Angostura Bitters	few drops of Angostura Bitters
ice cubes	ice cubes

Pour the tonic water into four glasses and stir a few drops of Angostura Bitters into each glass.

Add ice and serve.
Serves 4
Total Calories 40
10 Calories per portion

Iced Coffee

METRIC/IMPERIAL	AMERICAN
1.2 litres/2 pints fresh, strong black coffee	5 cups fresh, strong black coffee
few drops liquid sweetener, if required	few drops liquid sweetener, if required
crushed ice	crushed ice
1 scoop low-calorie ice cream	1 scoop low-calorie ice cream

Sweeten the coffee if needed, then chill well in the refrigerator. Just before serving, pour into glasses over crushed ice. Top each glass with ice cream.
Serves 6
Total Calories 30 Calories per scoop ice cream
30 Calories per portion

Fresh Herb Tea

METRIC/IMPERIAL	AMERICAN
1 pot freshly made hot tea	1 pot freshly made hot tea
few sprigs fresh mint, sage or camomile	few sprigs fresh mint, sage or camomile
liquid sweetener, if required	liquid sweetener, if required

Pour the tea over the herb in a heatproof glass. Add sweetener, if needed, then leave to infuse for a few minutes before serving.
Total Calories Negligible

Pineapple Jogger

METRIC/IMPERIAL	AMERICAN
1 × 440 g/15½ oz can pineapple in natural juice	1 × 15½ oz can pineapple in natural juice
150 ml/¼ pint plain yogurt	⅔ cup plain yogurt
4 tablespoons rosehip syrup	4 tablespoons rosehip syrup
300 ml/½ pint skimmed milk	1¼ cups skim milk

Put the pineapple and juice, yogurt and syrup into a blender or food processor and blend until smooth. Add the milk and blend until frothy. Pour into glasses and serve.
Serves 4
Total Calories 610
152 Calories per portion

Winter Warmer

METRIC/IMPERIAL	AMERICAN
300 ml/½ pint skimmed milk	1¼ cups skim milk
1 teaspoon cocoa or coffee powder	1 teaspoon unsweetened cocoa or coffee powder
few drops rum essence	few drops rum extract
liquid sweetener	liquid sweetener

Reserve 2 tablespoons milk and bring the remainder to the boil in a small saucepan. Place the cocoa or coffee in a mug, add the reserved milk and blend to form a smooth paste. Pour over the boiling milk, then add the essence (extract) and sweetener to taste. This is a soothing drink for winter evenings.
Serves 1
Total Calories 110 using cocoa powder
Total Calories 100 using coffee powder

Tomato Health Drink

METRIC/IMPERIAL	AMERICAN
1 × 425 g/15 oz can tomatoes	1 × 15 oz can tomatoes
50 g/2 oz Edam cheese, grated	½ cup grated Edam cheese
½ onion, chopped	½ onion, chopped
1 celery stick, chopped	1 stalk celery, chopped
½ green pepper, cored, seeded and chopped	½ green pepper, cored, seeded and chopped
salt	salt
freshly ground black pepper	freshly ground black pepper

Place all the ingredients in a blender or food processor and blend for approximately 1 minute, until smooth. Add salt and pepper to taste and dilute with water, if necessary.
Serves 6
Total Calories 260
43 Calories per portion

Mock Whisky

METRIC/IMPERIAL	AMERICAN
1 litre/1¾ pints low-calorie ginger ale	4¼ cups low-calorie ginger ale
4 tablespoons low-calorie lime juice	4 tablespoons low-calorie lime juice
ice cubes	ice cubes

Pour the ginger ale into four glasses and stir 1 tablespoon lime juice into each glass.
Add ice and serve.
Serves 4
5 Calories per portion

West Indian Cooler

METRIC/IMPERIAL	AMERICAN
250 ml/8 fl oz unsweetened orange juice	1 cup unsweetened orange juice
250 ml/8 fl oz unsweetened pineapple juice	1 cup unsweetened pineapple juice
ice cubes	ice cubes
soda water	soda water

Pour the orange and pineapple juices equally into four glasses, so that they are about half full.
Add ice and top up with soda water.
Serves 4
40 Calories per portion

Apple Aperitif

METRIC/IMPERIAL	AMERICAN
600 ml/1 pint iced tea	2½ cups iced tea
600 ml/1 pint clear sparkling apple juice	2½ cups clear sparkling apple juice
150 ml/¼ pint lemon juice	⅔ cup lemon juice
liquid sweetener	liquid sweetener
apple slices to decorate	apple slices to decorate

Mix the tea, apple juice and lemon juice together and add sweetener to taste. Serve well chilled, decorated with apple slices.
Serves 10
Total Calories 225
22 Calories per portion

Tropical Fruit Cup

METRIC/IMPERIAL	AMERICAN
300 ml/½ pint tropical fruit juice	1¼ cups tropical fruit juice
4 tablespoons lemon juice	4 tablespoons lemon juice
300 ml/½ pint soda water or sparkling mineral water	1¼ cups soda water or sparkling mineral water
dash of rum (optional)	dash of rum (optional)
dash of Angostura Bitters	dash of Angostura Bitters
crushed ice	crushed ice
To decorate:	**To decorate:**
slices of fruit	slices of fruit
sprigs of mint	sprigs of mint
4 cherries	4 cherries

Mix all the ingredients together and chill well in the refrigerator. Serve in tall glasses decorated with fresh fruit, mint and cherries.
Serves 4
Total Calories 170
42 Calories per portion

Spiced Coffee

METRIC/IMPERIAL	AMERICAN
1.2 litres/2 pints fresh black coffee	5 cups fresh black coffee
grated rind of 1 orange	grated rind of 1 orange
pinch of grated nutmeg	pinch of grated nutmeg
liquid sweetener	liquid sweetener
ice cubes to serve	ice cubes to serve

Mix the coffee with the orange rind and nutmeg and add sweetener to taste. Leave to infuse and chill in the refrigerator. Strain and serve in tall glasses with ice.
Serves 6
Total Calories Negligible

Chocolate Mandarin Whizz

METRIC/IMPERIAL	AMERICAN
1 × 298 g/10 oz mandarins in natural juice	1 × 10 oz can mandarins in natural juice
150 ml/¼ pint plain yogurt	⅔ cup plain yogurt
2 eggs	2 eggs
2 teaspoons drinking chocolate or malt milk powder	2 teaspoons drinking chocolate or malt milk powder

Put all the ingredients into a blender or food processor and blend until smooth. Pour into glasses and serve immediately.
Serves 4
Total Calories 400
100 Calories per portion

INDEX

ACKNOWLEDGEMENTS

The publishers would like to thank the following
photographers:
Bryce Attwell 11; Rex Bamber 2-3; Melvin Grey 6, 39;
Robert Golden 22, 27, 42, 55; Gina Harris 14, 34;
Verner Morgan 19; Grant Symon 31, 50, 58.
Ilustrations by Lindsay Blow.